Strangers at Home and Abroad

Strangers at Home and Abroad

Recollections of Austrian Jews Who Escaped Hitler

Edited by
ADI WIMMER

TRANSLATED BY EWALD OSERS

McFarland & Company, Inc., Publishers
Jefferson, North Carolina, and London

Library of Congress Cataloguing-in-Publication Data

Strangers at home and abroad : recollections of Austrian
    Jews who escaped Hitler / edited by Adi Wimmer ; translated
    by Ewald Osers.
        p.   cm.
    Includes bibliographical references and index.   ∞
    ISBN 0-7864-0668-2 (library binding : 50# alkaline paper)
    1. Jews — Austria — Biography.   2. Holocaust, Jewish
(1939–1945) — Personal narratives.   3. Antisemitism —
Austria.   4. Austria — Ethnic relations.   5. Austria —
Biography.   6. Refugees, Jewish — Austria — Biography.
I. Wimmer, Adi.   II. Title.
DS135.A93 A185   2000
943.6'004924'0092 — dc21
[B]   99-54798

British Library Cataloguing-in-Publication data are available

Manufactured in the United States of America

*McFarland & Company, Inc., Publishers
    Box 611, Jefferson, North Carolina 28640
    www.mcfarlandpub.com*

For Irene.
Without her support, this volume
would not have been possible.

Table of Contents

Part III. War and Exile

Introduction

The Background of 1988

This volume is one of many consequences of Austria's "Year of Recollection," or *Gedenkjahr,* as it was called. Throughout 1988, many historians, politicians, organizations, and media took a hard look at Austria's merger with Hitler's Germany in March of 1938. So did university professors, and with good reason. Prior to 1938, Austrian universities had been hotbeds of German nationalism. There were numerous vicious attacks against Jewish students (see Benno Weiser Varon or Sir Ernst Gombrich, in this volume), but the professors looked the other way. By their silence, they encouraged the attacks. In the run-up to 1988, there was a consensus among Austrian professors, particularly by those working in the humanities, that we must never again fail to speak out against the dangers of intolerance or racism. My contribution would be to secure the survival of oral reports by Austrian victims of Nazi persecution. Because so few of them returned to Austria after 1945, I had to find them in their countries of exile.

I started collecting these memoirs in 1987. First, I solicited written reports. Later, armed with two tape recorders, I traveled to Great Britain, the U.S.A. and Israel in order to meet the exiles in person and to conduct interviews. Much pain is present in their tales. So much pain that I was anxious to conclude this volume with one or two narratives that include positive views on Austria and Austrians. Of course I had no wish to diminish in any way the enormity of the crimes that were committed against Austrian Jews. Nor did I wish to divert from these crimes by pointing an accusing finger at the conditions which many refugees found in their host countries. Some of those interviewed reacted with enthusiasm to my project. They had been waiting for 50 years for an Austrian to show interest in their lives and concern for what they had gone through. Understandably, there was also some suspicion of my motives. Why was I interested in them? many asked. What was it all about? Would I, for instance, receive money or bonus points for my research record? And didn't the whole enterprise come far too late?

I do not think it is too late to attempt to make exile narratives part of our collective awareness. A democratic future needs an approach to the past which neither silences nor renders invisible the ordinary citizen. In the last two decades we have witnessed growing support for this demand, which may explain the shift in historical research towards the "worm's eye view," towards the everyday and oral history. Such a shift is particularly justified as regards the history of marginalized groups, such as ethnic minorities or social underdogs. My interest lies in Jewish exiles. They were forced to leave Austria after it submitted itself to Hitler in 1938. To my own and my country's shame, they were not invited back home after 1945. Until recently, as far as Austria's public awareness was concerned, they had no history. For decades after the war there was no public discussion of the meaning and significance of this particular chapter in our history. As we denied to outsiders and repressed within ourselves any Austrian involvement in the horrors of Nazism, we were left no option but to repress the existence of roughly 130,000 of our fellow Austrians in exile. Accepting the mere fact of their existence (let alone welcoming them home) would have meant assigning them a role in a public discourse which we did our best *not* to have. Thus, to gather for our own collective memory and to "unerase" the experiences of a steadily thinning group of people is a task of urgency as well as moral necessity. The recollections of former Austrians gathered in this volume are thus to be seen first and foremost as a contribution towards an improved culture of memory.

That there is a grossly deficient "culture of memory" in Austria was made painfully clear by the Waldheim scandal of 1986. (Kurt Waldheim, Austrian president, 1986–1992, was elected despite his former Nazi affiliation and alleged involvement in the deportation of Jews.) His election to the post of president of the nation was less of a shock than the accompanying resurgence of views which we thought had been overcome with the death of Nazism. In Austria, writing letters to the editors of newspapers is something of a national pastime, but the Waldheim case produced an unprecedented deluge of letters. What I read in literally dozens of them was: Do we *really* have to look at the history of Nazism yet again — who needs it? Others were more aggressive, writing, "We will apologize for the crimes that were committed in the name of National Socialism only after the English apologize for Dresden, for their colonial wars and the repression in Ireland, and the Americans for the extermination of the Native Americans, their imperialism in Central America, and for Vietnam."

Meanwhile we have had the 60-year anniversary of Austria's annexation in 1938, which has ruptured, but not totally destroyed, the veil of our collective amnesia. But things are far from satisfactory, and from time to time we find renewed causes for concern. For instance, according to a poll taken in October 1991, 86 percent of Austrians grossly overestimate the number of Austrian Jews.[1] Moreover, 19 percent think there should be Jewish quotas for certain professions such as doctors or lawyers, seven percent said they feel physically uncomfortable in the presence of Jews, and a full 50 percent think Jews share some of the responsibility for the Holocaust. Evidently Austria's political culture still leaves much to be desired. In my view we can identify as one factor causing this depressing state of affairs a simple ignorance of what really happened to Austrian Jews in 1938 — on a private, physical, individual plane. Once people have made the effort to find out how the forces of history trickle down and shape — or destroy — individual lives, they will resist the lure of simple abstractions and defamatory prejudices. On the level of individual lives we find a surprising richness of Viennese types, giving the lie to both the stereotype of the "rich Jewish bankers" and the "Viennese Nazi beasts." Indubitably, as an Austrian, to accept the challenge of remembrance is to risk pain. And yet I was surprised by how few of the testimonies I gathered speak of unmitigated scorn and unhealed pain, how notably absent were views of a collective Austrian guilt — despite the very real horrors in those testimonies. Maybe because there were so few acts of humanity, those that *did* occur are remembered with exceptional intensity and gratitude. Occasionally I was dumbfounded by the generosity of my narrators, how they made excuses for their fellow Viennese who did nothing to help. One such generous view that I repeatedly heard was: "If I hadn't been born Jewish, how do I know I wouldn't have joined the Nazis myself?" My generation is usually much harsher in its judgments on Nazis than the generation of Nazi victims, and meeting these victims has taught me humility.

How Long Does Exile Last?

We know almost everything there is to know about the events which led to the annexation of Austria by Hitler's Germany in March 1938. We also know the cost of these events to the Austrian economy. We even know the cost of the subsequent devastations of World War II. A lot less is known about that history as seen through the eyes of its victims, however, and almost no research has been done about the *psychological* cost of suddenly becoming a second-class citizen, of the subsequent banishment and the years of involuntary exile. The situation is exacerbated by the fact that much valuable research by Austrian historians (also literary historians) has simply been ignored by the public. There has been no appreciable improvement in the mass-media debate about the year 1938 and its victims. Occasionally a high-minded individual will make the gallant effort to repopularize such concepts as "mastering the past" or "the labor of mourning," but the typical Austrian response to demands like these is a beery "so what?" Worse still, certain political factions are busily engaged in metamorphosing the erstwhile criminals into victims and the Nazi crimes into "fate," which happens to have been one of Hitler's favorite words. In October 1990, the leader of a radical Austrian right-wing party which, incredibly, won 22 percent of the vote in the November 1995 elections, declared (at an annual meeting of SS veterans) that "nobody who ever wore a German uniform has any reason to be ashamed of his service"—*and there was no public outcry.* These are frightening points of contact between the past and the present where one kind of exile ends and another one begins. Which, one wonders, was harder to bear? The first, which offered a glimmer of hope once the Nazis had been defeated, or the subsequent one, which brought only the depressing realization that there would be no apologies, no remorse, no compensation — and thus an everlasting alienation? The poet Alfred Polgar came to this bitter conclusion in 1949: *Die Fremde ist nicht Heimat geworden. Aber die Heimat Fremde* ("The foreign country did not become a home. But home became foreign"). Theodor Kramer, the talented young poet whose career was brutally destroyed by the Nazis, and who limped back to Vienna in 1956 merely to die six months later, wrote this coda for one of his final poems: "It is only at home that I am eternally foreign."

At this point I hope to be excused if I give vent to one of my incessant irritations. If the research into the achievements of exiled Jewish scientists, writers and artists has found lamentably little response in the public domain, then the "response" to the stories of ordinary exiles has been a crushing indifference. Until the early 1990s, no academic researchers, no public institutions and no politicians expressed the slightest interest in them. Austria did not so much "marginalize" its exiles; it erased them from its collective awareness. We need only to look to our political neighbor in the north to see that in postwar Europe this was not the norm. In Germany, most cities have made it their task to invite, little by little, *all* of their former Jewish citizens back home for at least a few days (all expenses paid, of course), and there is ample public and private support for such gestures of atonement. But what of Austria? In 1990 I suggested to the city of Baden (a prosperous resort near Vienna) that it should invite two ex–Badeners, one living in Jerusalem, the other in Reading, England, to spend some days in their birthtown as a gesture of atonement. I received a letter from the mayor of Baden, who was plainly irritated by my attempt to "interfere" in the "internal affairs" of Baden: The city would invite its own guests, he wrote, but right now there was no money for that sort of extravaganza, and anyway, he continued, the city had just restored the old synagogue, which clearly demonstrated the liberal attitudes of the city fathers. Regrettably, there are hardly any Jews left in Baden, but the building has been turned into a tourist showpiece. This is a fairly typical Austrian response, I fear: There is money to restore the damage in Jewish buildings (because the results become tourist showpieces), but no money to restore the terrible damage in Jewish minds and souls.

A case in point is the story of Edward Arie, one of this book's narrators. In June 1991 it came to his notice that Austria had amended its 1946 law on paying indemnity to victims of Nazism. Mr. Arie had been denounced by a workmate and arrested the day after the November 9, 1938, pogrom. He suffered the usual gleeful SS tortures, and then spent seven weeks at the concentration camp of Dachau, where he almost perished. He was released thanks to the unflagging efforts of his sister and fiancée, and on condition that he not tell *anyone* about life in the camp (which he, as a traumatized inmate, actually kept secret until several years after the war was over). Luckily, he and his later wife got out in time, but his father did not. Fifty-three years later it seemed as if Austria was willing to compensate him. After seven months of working on his application, the authorities came to the following decision: No compensation is payable for the death of Mr. Arie's father, as Mr. Arie was already over 18 at the time of the father's death; and the adequate compensation for the seven weeks at Dachau should be 1.720 schillings, roughly $150. Edward Arie returned the insulting check with a polite note. A year later he died, and the thought that this kind, unblemished man went to the grave without receiving justice from my country has haunted me ever since.

In the face of such unspeakable stinginess the lavish receptions given to all of the *famous* Jewish exiles becomes another source of irritation. From Ernst Gombrich such treatment elicited a somewhat pained comment: "Later on, Austria awarded all sorts and manners of orders and distinctions to me." VIPs such as Teddy Kollek (the retired mayor of Jerusalem), Billy Wilder, Frederic Morton and Lord Weidenfeld have all been fêted and wooed by the Austrian authorities. After the Waldheim debacle, our politicians badly needed the photo-ops to polish up their "liberal" image. The stark contrast between the popularity of a few and the indifference toward the mass of exiles is an aspect of that anti–Semitic groundswell we can trace back to someone like the late–19th century mayor of Vienna, Lueger. When reproached by some friends because, in spite of his anti–Semitic speeches, he still dined with rich Jews, Lueger coined the memorable phrase *Wer a Jud is, bestimm i* (*"Only I* will decide who is a Jew."*)

On Austrian Jews
That Did Not Return

When in 1945 the Nazi nightmare seemed to be over, many of the Jews expelled by the denizens of the *Ostmark* (the Nazi name for Austria) were faced with the question of whether to return. Because of the devastations, an immediate return often was not possible. But as the months and years passed, two things became apparent. On the federal, state and local levels alike, the "de-nazified" administrations had little interest in inviting Jews back and were not going to allocate any means for such a morally inspired venture. The solitary exception was a communist city councilor of Vienna, Viktor Matejka, who was ousted after a few months in office. Secondly, Austrians showed a chameleon-like ability to change their colors. Those who in 1938 had learned overnight to shout "Heil Hitler" instead of "Heil Schuschnigg," as Stefan Zweig remarked in his autobiography,[2] were once again converted. After years of collaboration with Nazism, they effortlessly constructed an anti–Nazi self-image without ever confronting their involvement in the evils of the past. Miraculously they would change into "the first victims of Nazism," who had suffered both under the Nazis and from the liberation. The Austrian poet Alfred Polgar, himself an exile, writing in *The Emigrant and His Homeland,* observed:

> There is a Faust-fragment by Lessing, in which the ghost, asked "What is the fastest thing on earth?" replies, "The transition from good to evil."

> Proof for the correctness of this reply was offered a few years ago by the incomprehensible rapidity with which crosses turned into hooked crosses, and men into beasts. Now and at the same speed we witnessed the retransition.[3]

In "hundreds of letters" (as Hermann Broch claimed), and fairly regularly during their first visit to Vienna after 1945, returning Jews searching for their murdered relatives ran into a miasma of self-pity coupled with an aggressive denial of guilt. "How smart it was of you, Herr Rosenbaum, to emigrate," they would say. "As usual, you Jews were more clever than we. Oh, you have no idea how terribly we suffered." Broch agonized about the decision to return until death took that choice out of his hands. When Hilde Spiel (having left before the Anschluss, she escaped the traumatizing effects of the street terror) returned to Vienna in early 1946 and the headwaiter of her café made exactly this type of remark, her reaction was one of uncomprehending disgust:

> Expropriation, humiliation, arrest and mortal danger, illegal border-crossings, the years of exile as an "enemy alien," surviving in a country badly disrupted by war — all of it would count for nothing, would vanish in thin air, dissolved by a snapping of two fingers.[4]

And while a mere three years after the end of the war journals and newspapers were full of Wehrmacht "heroism stories," stories of *real* heroism, such as hiding Jews from the marauding Nazis, were not considered worth printing. Alfred Polgar, conceding that the months of allied bombing must have been hard, wrote: "But to accuse the dawn of the day for its greyish light ill befits those who found their bearings so comfortably well in the pitch blackness that preceded it."[5] Hardly anyone was able to remember, wrote Broch in a letter:

> The human memory is incredibly short, especially in relation to its own errors and misdemeanors, and that is why man is capable of constantly lying to himself. Of those many decent and well-behaved folks whom you meet today, more than half, in my view, were decent and well-behaved Hitler-screamers who no longer recall that fact.[6]

Dr. [Georg] Lexer, a prominent surgeon in my hometown of Klagenfurt, had a firsthand experience of this kind. In 1938, he was 15 and an ardent supporter of Austria's prime minister, Dr. Kurt Schuschnigg. When Schuschnigg ordered a plebiscite for March 13 on the question of whether to amalgamate Austria with Germany (which Hitler claimed was the fervent wish of all Austrians) or to stay independent, he and a close friend were busy distributing anti–Hitler leaflets. A few days after Austria's demise Lexer was thunderstruck when he saw his pal once again distributing leaflets, *Nazi* leaflets this time. "How can you," he confronted him, "campaign for the Nazis when only last week we two campaigned against them?" The friend fixed him with cold eyes. "If you repeat that lie ever again, you *Saujud,* I'll kick your teeth in."[7] The speed with which the former friend had changed his colors and manipulated his memory was perhaps remarkable, but there were tens of thousands who "discovered" that they had always been supporters of Nazism. And after 1945, the same mechanism worked once again. In a diary entry of October 1950 Günther Anders not only reveals the horrible reality of an unrepentant Vienna, but offers a psychological explanation for memory loss of this kind:

> Even after the murder of six million Jews they dare ... to make Jews their scapegoat again, this time the accidental remaining Jew, the accidental survivor. Not the batterer is guilty — presumably he really does not recall his murders — but the battered: because he alone cannot forget the beating, the batterer and the battered.[8]

Quite "ordinary" survivors will also eloquently express anger with and alienation from their mother country. As one of my interviewees wryly remarked: "Oh those Austrians will never forgive me for the fact that they sent me to Dachau"—the infamous concentration camp to the west of Munich. New myths about stupendous Jewish privileges sprang up at the beer tables all across Austria. Dare I admit that I found such a prejudice in my own family, as late as in 1993? A close relative, a devout Catholic who is commonly called a "decent person." While watching the television news one night — there was a report on repressive Israeli policies towards Palestinians — she suddenly exclaimed, "Those damn Jews can get away with anything!" Shocked, I pointed at the wider historical picture, and how inappropriate it was particularly of us Austrians to express such views. And out came the slurs, one by one: They had rewritten history. They had far too much power. We had paid them enough. We were still paying them horrendous sums of money, a fact that was hushed up, a conspiracy. Didn't I know the sole reason why Herr Meinl (he is the owner of a chain of quality food stores found all over Austria) was not passing his business on to his son? Such a move would eliminate the company's privilege, granted to all Jewish businessmen who had returned after 1945, of not paying any income tax for the duration of their lives!

But why should I be astounded by such bizarre stories, when the founding fathers of the Second Republic, as we now know, behaved in no less callous a manner?[9]

The Difference Between Emigration and Exile

Distinguishing between "exile" and such related concepts as "emigration/émigré," "displaced person," "foreigner" or "alien" and "refugee" does matter in a context of traumatized vs. nontraumatized writing. "Emigration" I define as the conscious decision, usually arrived at through years of deliberation and angst, to abandon one country for another. The two main reasons for emigration are a hope for better economic conditions and (though less frequently) an absence of political freedom. Emigration is always accompanied by subtle identity changes, anteceding the actual uprooting, which are initiated by the émigré himself. Why? In order to justify to oneself and to friends and family the extraordinary decision of giving up the certainty of home in exchange for a great uncertainty of the future, the émigré has to loosen his emotional ties to the motherland. It becomes necessary to "disenthrall," as Emerson would have said, oneself of a cultural legacy. At the same time an image of the new country will be constructed, resulting in unrealistically benign and opportunity-filled notions. Separation from a regional or national identity is thus a prolonged process easing the pain of leaving. Subsequently, the emigrant will work extremely hard to be a success. The emigrant needs the success in order to validate emigration, to prove to himself *and to everyone who stayed behind* that the decision was correct. The emigrant thus often becomes a model citizen, fiercely loyal and patriotic, even more so than his peers of older families. An instructive example is provided by Ron Kovic, the paraplegic Vietnam veteran and author of *Born on the Fourth of July*. The night before joining the Marines he stays up watching television until "The Star-Spangled Banner" plays: "I put my hand over my heart and stood rigid at attention until the screen went blank."[10] A Jewish immigrant remembers the same emotion on the occasion of being awarded American citizenship:

> We practically waltzed out of the building. We were citizens again! American citizens! We were practically like everyone else. We felt

superpatriotic. Five years after our arrival, we only spoke English at home.... We celebrated every American holiday. We all felt entirely American and did everything we could to support the country.... We had no past.[11]

Yet another term that confuses our discussion is "expatriation." Expatriation differs in that the causes of migration are less economic than cultural. The typical expatriate is an artist who is disenchanted with the narrow-mindedness and sterility of his environment. Beckett, Joyce, Ernest Hemingway, the restless Rainer Maria Rilke, E.M. Remarque after 1945, the Australians Christina Stead, Miles Franklin, and Patrick White for long stretches of their lives, were all "expats." But the expatriate does not necessarily expect a more prosperous life, seeking a *freer* life instead. Nor is the expat beholden to praise his host country. However, what the émigré and the expat have in common is that they can return home at any time. The choice is always possible, and frequently the return happens at the point when success and financial security are no longer in doubt.

But what about the term "exile"? Bertolt Brecht, who fled from Nazi persecution as early as 1933 and who fled in the return direction in 1945, this time from HUAC (House Un-American Activities Committee) persecution, thought the distinction between the terms "émigré" and "exile" important enough to devote a whole poem, "Über die Bezeichnung Emigranten" ["On the Term Emigrants"], to it.[12]

It is here that a radical difference becomes apparent. Exile is not chosen, it is forced upon. Whether a return to one's country of origin will ever be possible hangs in doubt. When the exile compares his former status as a respected citizen with that of a refugee in an alien land, he will be shocked about a huge loss in quality of life. A great many Viennese Jews had been, in pre–1938 days, highly prosperous and respected. For instance, after the annexation a full 78 percent of the teaching staff of the medical faculty of Vienna University were dismissed, almost all of them Jews.[13] In the arts and sciences, as well as in trade and commerce, Jews were present at a disproportionately high rate. Overnight they became nonpersons whom everyone was free to molest, to rob, even to lynch. Shocking as it is in retrospect, Viennese anti–Semitism turned out to be more brutal than the anti–Semitism of Hitler-Germany up until 1938. Moreover, whereas anti–Semitism in Germany was very much the domain of bureaucrats, in Vienna it was acted out like popular "street theatre" with gleeful audience participation. Harassing the Jews was a playful activity, carried out by the gemütlich Viennese in a three-quarter beat. Quite precipitately, any reliable social consensus for living among others vanished. There were no norms and rules anymore, no law that would protect. As one of my interviewees remembered, "It was as though we had been thrown into an impenetrable jungle together with wild animals, and we had no weapons with which to defend ourselves." Dozens of people would disappear, as they still disappear today in certain Latin American dictatorships, without anyone knowing where, but also without anyone asking questions about these disappearances. There was, of course, organized terror carried out by the SA and the SS —*Austrian* SA and SS mind you — which made Theodor Kramer speak of Vienna as located by the beautiful brown Danube. But it seems that the mass of *private* examples of petty nastiness have an even more prominent place in the memories of exiles, *and it is these memories which have been so demoralizing.* Many spoke in apocalyptic terms of the outrages that happened to them, using images of collapse and chaos, but also imparting terrifying insights. Because of the precipitateness of all the changes, the soon-to-be exiles could not find the time to properly assess, analyze and understand a multitude of processes affecting their lives and identities. It was as though they were shock-frozen. And indeed Lore Segal writes in these terms in her autobiography, *Other People's Houses:*

> "When am I going?" I asked. "Thursday," my father said. The day after tomorrow. Then I felt the icy chill below my chest where my insides had been.[14]

Benno Weiser Varon, using a similar metaphor, speaks of the Anschluss as "the beginning of the Stone Age of the heart,"[15] whereas Max Knight, coauthor of the "duography" entitled *One and One Make Three,* makes a reference to a cultural abortion when he writes that fleeing Vienna was leaving "the womb of my home in Vienna, my family, my country, my tradition and security. It was a violent birth, Hitler as midwife."[16] Many exiles had recurring dreams; some have them to this day. One example is offered by Caroline Weintraub in this book. Mrs. Edith Arie dreamt "at least fifty times, maybe a hundred" the following dream: "Suddenly there is an order to leave within two minutes. Frantically I begin to pack a suitcase, except I do not know what to pack and what to leave, and so I leave the house with an empty case. In the streets I do not know where to go, and so I ask the people, "Where do I go?" and they ask me back, "Where d'you WANT to go?" and I say, "I do not know, all I know is that I have to GO, can you tell me where?" and they all laugh and leave me standing there. And the streets through which I hurry are suddenly all alien to me, I do not know where I am, and I do not recognize any faces, and I am terrified that I will not make the deadline and that they will come for me. When I wake up, I am soaked in sweat, and for a few seconds I never know where I am."[17]

Finally, a terrifying dream connoting the loneliness of exiles who had to leave all their friends and family to the Holocaust. The narrator was "buying garden chairs, all sorts, and then all kinds, and then, while the salesman counted up, she said to him: 'And when shall you deliver the people who shall occupy them?'"[18]

Understanding Exile Narratives as Narratives of Trauma

Our time has made traveling so easy. Many of us have become not only accomplished travelers, but semioticians of alien cultures. We know how to read the signs, we love the differences of the sights, the sounds, the smells. There is sensuality in our journeys. But who has ever tried to imagine the feelings of teenagers arriving all alone and against their will in a new country, not to spend a vacation but to stay there, maybe forever? What terror must have been in their hearts as they watched an alien, drab landscape, unfamiliar houses or street signs that yielded no meaning; what incomprehension may have filled their souls as they were unable to read the faces of foster parents, teachers, policemen? The new arrivals were, in a symbolic sense, naked. As the writer Lion Feuchtwanger wrote of his New York exile in 1941, "I feel like a primitive from the jungle who sees telegraph poles and wires. He knows that these wires have a function, but he has no idea which."[19] Although we know that there existed a great deal of goodwill in England, France, and other countries that accepted Jews, some people and authorities were less than perfect. Thus the British Central Office for Refugees (commonly known as Bloomsbury House) issued a flyer to all refugees from Nazism advising them about their behavior. "Don't talk German in the streets, in public places or any places where others may hear you," it said, which must have given them the impression that the British might mob them in the streets. "Don't ask whether your friends and relatives can be brought into the country, whether or not they have permits," it went on, addressing their main sorrow, since *everybody* had been separated from their beloved. "Do be as quiet and modest as possible" was another and somewhat ominous remark. Ending on an uplifting note, it had the eminently practical advice "Do be as cheerful as possible."[20] The writer of such a pamphlet clearly had very little idea of the unspeakable pain characterizing every day of the new arrivals. (Indeed the whole British government seems to have firmly shut its eyes against the terror of Hitler's Germany against its Jewish citizens. "Peace in our time" was its vain hope; and one needed to see Hitler as a "gentleman," not as a thug, in order to continue the ill-fated policy of appeasement.)

Maybe we need to relate trauma problems of exiled persons to events closer to our own time. Reading an article describing the traumas of Bosnian war refugees now being treated in Zagreb, I was struck by a number of parallels.

> Displaced persons represent a group which has been struck with cumulative impact of stress. Their well-being, mental and physical health, and their social position have all been imperilled at the same time. Seeing no end to their exile, horrified by the irrationality of destruction, overcome with disbelief and astonishment of the hatred of their former friends and fellow citizens, they are faced with identity crisis. All that has been built into the foundations of the concept of self: job, family, friends, home, aims and values, has been exposed to destruction and ruin.[21]

Exactly the same is true as regards the cataclysmic changes experienced by Austrian Jews. Even those who were not forced to scrub the streets, who did not run the gauntlet of jeering hordes of anti–Semites, must have been terrorized by the sudden emergence of thousands of swastikas, those menacing symbols of hatred and death: on flags, on the arms of ordinary citizens, in shops. As one lady recalled, every day she had to pass her beloved Vienna Opera House, which displayed a huge banner reading: "Jewishness is Crime" (*Judentum ist Verbrechertum*).

Even if we comprehend the sudden vulnerability of self and property, we do not yet know the whole story. All certainties regarding one's life and career were stripped away. Moreover, the certainties of a static society were much sought after by the ordinary citizen, much more so than in our time, as Stefan Zweig points out in his autobiography. There was a strict sequence of rites and events denoting maturity or progress which had been tacitly agreed upon by society. For example, there had to be an engagement ceremony before marriage, professional training and the first career steps before engagement, settling into an appropriate apartment before parenthood, and so on. Such steps and expectations were beyond dispute and could, in some cases, even be sued for. (Breaking an engagement was a civil offense; the aggrieved party could sue for damages.) Because of the Anschluss, all expectations of a foreseeable life development were disrupted. Not to be disregarded is the fact that personal relationships are not the only ones of a biographical validity: relations with business partners or clients are of relevance, too. When they were removed, self-esteem and social status were grievously injured. Significantly, the number of male suicides was more than ten times as high as that of women. In rare cases, life in exile was gradually reconstructed and a prewar standard of living achieved. But even then the expectations of a normal Jewish life, with its strong emphasis on the relations of an extended family, could not be fulfilled. Ceremonies such as a bar mitzvah or a wedding were incomplete because, well, because aunts and uncles and grandparents and friends and neighbors had not survived the brown pestilence. Even the use of the mother tongue was problematic. Writer Fritz Beer remembers: "I was no longer allowed to remain loyal to a language dwelled in by the barbarians."[22] He revised his decision, but others did not. I know of cases in which marriage partners (both of them German-speaking) quarreled about which language to use in the home.

In contrast to the refugees of the Bosnian war, Jewish refugees were soon needed by their host countries (Britain in particular) in the general effort to win the war. No one was keener than they to share the inclemencies of shortages, blackouts and long hours of work. But the wartime attitude of "grinning and bearing" breaks down sooner or later, and then what? Do the narratives find an outlet, and if so, do they get an audience? And even if they do, does this cure the trauma? From the study of other genres of trauma literature, such as war narratives, holocaust narratives, rape and incest narratives, we know that this is far from assured. A study of Hiroshima survivors, for example, has revealed that 30 years after the fact they feel deeply guilty about their survival and that they are defenseless against the ostracism of the get-ahead postwar Japanese generation, which has largely rendered their plight invisible.[23] Incest victims need on average 15 years between the crime and the telling of the crime.[24] Holocaust survivors such as Eli Wiesel and Simon Wiesenthal have both testified to their own "survivor guilt" as well as to long public indifference to their tales. Wiesel moreover has argued that nontraumatized readers tend to read holocaust literature as allegories or metaphors for the human existence rather than concrete historical fact. The Anschluss has similarly not found many literary champions or publishers: until very recently, it tended to get glossed over both by contemporary Austrian literature *and* our collective memory. In England and the U.S.A., only a few brave publishers risked their money on Anschluss memoirs. As far as the general public is concerned, I have often heard the story that, owing to the seductive "schmaltzyness" of certain movies, many English or American citizens didn't even believe the horror stories of exiled Austrian Jews. There is the well-known case of *The Sound of Music*, which presents a totally misleading picture of prewar Austria, but even Charlie Chaplin's *The Great Dictator* (1942) inexplicably portrays "Ostarik" as a neighboring country offering refuge to persecuted Jews.

An even more important aspect was a self-generated censorship of exiles. Their suffering, so they felt with some justification, had been *negligible* in comparison with the horrors of the Holocaust, and so many thought it inappropriate to fuss over their losses. The result was decades of silence and suppression. To me it seems that this was particularly strong as a syndrome in Israel. Israel was quick to establish a culture of memory, as was only fitting for a state that might have never come into being without the Holocaust. But while the horrors of the mass extermination were meticulously documented, scant attention was given to the traumas of those who had been expelled. *You are the lucky ones* was drummed into them: *You must be glad to be here. You have an obligation to be happy.* Guiltily, the ones who had gotten out in time agreed. But often remained quietly unhappy and homesick.

As Julia Kristeva has argued, there is a great need to rejoin those seemingly mutually exclusive areas of "longing" and "knowing."[25] In the final phase of life, as family ties, friendships, and business contacts fall by the wayside, it is natural to seek a reconciliation with those who never asked for forgiveness. This becomes even more plausible considering a certain disenchantment with host countries: the colder social climate brought about by Thatcherism, alarmingly high crime rate, or the disintegration of American cities are often cited in this context. Stella Rotenberg, who started writing verse at the age of 50 and has since turned into an accomplished poet, wrote one of the most moving exile poems that I know. It is entitled "Rückkehr" ("Return"), and lists a number of nonreasons for returning to Austria, such as the (clichéd) notions of an atmosphere, gemütlichkeit, the waltzes, the crystal snow in winter. The final stanza explains in stunning simplicity: "Simply/ in order to hear the sound of my mother tongue/ once more, would I return/ into the abyss of hell."[26] This is not an inflated metaphor: The city that murdered your mother deserves such an image. "Once bitten, twice shy," as an old proverb knows.

I am reminded of an Austrian television program screened in 1993 in which a New York woman, interviewed by Austrian television about her feelings for Vienna said, "I would so much like to love this city again. But I daren't." In a more tortuous statement and playing on the multiple meanings of "to live," Dorit Whiteman's aunt explained: "You know I could no longer live in Vienna. But the only city where I could really *live* is Vienna — if I could only live there."

Still, the recovery of lost or suppressed aspects of personal identity can be a healing process. The notion of both personal and social healing is an important aspect in the public reception of trauma narratives. Like most forms of orthodox psychoanalysis, healing involves the passage from silence about troubling experiences to sorrow and story. When suffering is denied or repressed, it continues to affect the person trying to forget. Those who follow that path (and I have encountered such individuals) are often unaware that the sharing of an individual sorrow with an audience can have a beneficial social effect. The fact of the matter is that this audience is largely an English-speaking one. My original feeling was that my (Austrian) society, with its history of collective evil, badly needs to recall the stories of its victims into its collective memory. But later I realized that what the surviving Jewish victims of the Anschluss want more than anything else is that members of their adopted countries — friends, neighbors, descendants — know of their stories. Not just for selfish reasons, but to prevent such things from ever happening again. Since they have been such exemplary citizens of the U.S.A. or of Britain, are they not owed some attention? And who can doubt that in times of growing ethnic intolerance, their cautionary tales are both timely and instructive?

About Myself

I was born in 1949 in Braunau, Adolf Hitler's birthtown, and went to school there until my graduation in 1967. I was christened "Adolf," after my father. As a devout Catholic my father never supported Hitler. On the other hand, he did nothing to resist the régime: He was one of millions who thought it best to adjust to the new situation and to survive. There were no Jews in the rural area where he lived in 1938. Earlier, though, he had known some Jews living in Braunau. Three of them, to be precise. What happened to them? A shrug of the shoulders. After the war, did no one try to find out? Goodness, what an idea — there were more pressing problems. And after these had been solved and respectability had returned, it was apparently too late to be curious about three Jews who had once lived in the same city. Their traces are indeed now lost.

So my parents thought that, a mere four years after the war, naming their son "Adolf" did not carry any political meaning. They are representative examples for a generation that managed to forget Nazism in record time. In the 1950s, the past was still very visible: men hobbling on crutches, a neighbor who had only one arm — "cripples" we bluntly called them in our pre–politically correct times. And then the American soldiers riding around in jeeps and on trucks — how we kids all missed their sweets after Austria was demilitarized in the fall of 1955. There is one enduring memory about asking questions on the war: I would always be told that there was no point in talking about it "yet again." From the moment I was mature enough to ask I was told *not* to ask *yet again.* The answers had already been given; apparently, there was no more to say. As the years passed, this began to sound ever more plausible — but still there was no open discussion of the Nazi or war years in any of the major clearinghouses of information: the family, the school, the church. When in the wake of the Waldheim debacle I finally stood my ground and argued I had a right to know more about his activities in those years, my father was genuinely surprised and a tad offended that I should be so insistent. During my eight years of attending high school at Braunau, the activities of its most (in)famous son were never part of the regular syllabus. Occasionally we would raise an issue ourselves, and if our teachers reluctantly answered, they talked about National Socialism in terms that clearly located it *outside our own borders.* As Edward Said would say, National Socialism was constructed as "the Other," even though it had been very much part of Austria's collective identity a mere two decades earlier. A conspiracy of silence permeated our culture. For instance, there was a steady, but secret flow of tourists visiting Hitler's birthhouse; the tourists would usually ask youngsters like myself how to get there, as they were embarrassed to ask adults. And yet the issue of Hitler as Braunau's legacy was never debated. Is it possible that the adults did not know what we all did? As a 13-year-old I once accompanied a tourist to Hitler's birthhouse and watched with fascination as this elderly gentleman scraped some of the mortar off the wall into a paper bag. When I told this to a group of classmates, they all reciprocated with similar stories.

Another enduring memory: My history teacher, a bigoted Catholic, once began to make glassy-eyed speculations about the glorious future Braunau might have had "if we had only won the war."

Although there is much to be ashamed about in Austria's postwar history, it is primarily for selfish reasons that I explore the life stories of Nazi victims. If we only learn more about what really happened during the time of Hitler on the level of the sufferers, then we are better armed against a comeback of right-wing extremism. My teenage son once asked me, "How did Nazism and that business with the persecution of the Jews start?" Remembering what Asa Baber, a journalist and Vietnam veteran, had once said about the Vietnam War, I replied, "Very quietly. When it got noisy and more people took notice, it was already too late." But there is another reason. I firmly believe in the therapeutic quality of personal stories. When we encounter people of a different culture, a different language, of a different appearance, we tend to assume an attitude of defensiveness. We primarily perceive an "otherness" in them. The best way to break down the barrier we have created ourselves is to hear their stories.

The validity of such a strategy was proved in rather horrible ways by the outbreak of the Yugoslav Civil Wars in 1991, which have cost an estimated 250,000 lives. Politicians, historians, even artists were at a loss to explain why the people of a state who had peacefully lived together for almost 50 years would start shooting each other. The phrase "outbreak of ancient hatred" cropped up in many comments, but those using it were at a loss to explain why "ancient hatred" could kindle a brushfire of incomprehensible violence. Violence not just by uniformed soldiers, but by quite ordinary citizens. The truth surely is that in Yugoslavia, various cultures and peoples lived *side by side*, but not *with each other*. Stories of how since the Middle Ages the Croats and the Serbs, the Macedonians and the Slovenes, the Kosovo Albanians and the Bosnian Muslims had all suffered at the hands of another ethnic group were discouraged by an official policy that saw a regional brand of communism (called "Titoism") as the new bond uniting different ethnicities. I have had occasion to talk with many Bosnian and Croatian refugees in the past years, and it is always the same story: We did not really know them. We kept to our own kind. We were never brought together in discussion groups. It was considered seditious to talk of our historic conflicts, so we kept quiet. And when Tito had died and communism crumbled, there was nothing to stop the country's slide into collective barbarism. Had the citizens of the former Yugoslavia only been allowed to tell their stories to one another, they would have found out about a common bond of suffering. As it was, each group saw itself as the one that had suffered the most, and had to settle a score.

In a world witnessing the relentless rise of right-wing violence — this includes the United States — in a world that has largely eliminated wars between states but is helpless in preventing violent conflict *within* states (Somalia, Sudan, Mexico, Guatemala, Indonesia, Bosnia), personal stories that establish our common humanity are an indispensable tool in maintaining peaceful, civil conditions. Listening to the stories requires an effort, to be sure. But it is worth making.

Adi Wimmer
Klagenfurt, Austria
Fall 1999

PART I

Anti–Semitism
Before Hitler

Anton Walter Freud

Oxted, Surrey

Anton Walter Freud, born April 3, 1921, in Vienna. Grandson of Sigmund Freud. Escaped from Vienna with his father (Martin Freud) on May 15, 1938, via Paris to London. Completed his schooling at a private school in London in 1939. After starting university, interned, along with his father, in May 1940, first in Leicester prison then in a camp on the Isle of Man. In September 1940 shipped to Australia on board the *Dunera*. Together with some 20 other internees he returned by the first possible ship in October 1941 and joined the Pioneer Corps. At the beginning of 1943 volunteered for a special unit of the British army. In April 1945 participated in a parachute operation in Styria. Married, 1946 (3 children, 9 grandchildren). Demobilized in September 1946. Studied chemistry; after graduation, became a chemical engineer with several British firms, from 1976 freelance consultant. Retired 1985.

We certainly had so-called Aryan acquaintances, but no Aryan friends. And I had never been to an Aryan's home. I can recall only one instance of having invited an Aryan school friend to my home; his name was Harry Stöger, and his father owned a pub on Obere Donaustrasse. Only once, on a skiing holiday, did I make the acquaintance of an Aryan woman. We were on the Schmittenhöhe, near Zell am See, in the Austrian Alps, my father and myself. We made the acquaintance of two women, mother and daughter. Their name was Parkensamer. It was a totally harmless acquaintance; we once danced together at the four o'clock tea. But it left such an impression on me, the fact that I had a non–Jewish girlfriend or girl acquaintance, that I remember it to this day, more than 50 years later. All my girlfriends were Jewish, the friends or cousins of schoolmates.

I had no other opportunities. The same was true of my parents, aunts, and grandparents. There was apartheid as in South Africa. We were totally apart. But there were no laws about it; it was done automatically. One simply belonged to one's coreligionists, and this was accepted as a matter of course. No one tried to break out of this tight system. I too never questioned it — it always seemed entirely natural to me. A fish belongs in the water, a bird belongs in the air. We knew where we belonged.

But at that time, before the Anschluss, our relations with those other Austrians weren't bad at all, or, more accurately, there were no relations — except for the domestic servants, who, of course, were always Aryan. In point of fact, one only knew a small number. One also avoided anti–Semitic remarks. If one knew that a person was probably an anti–Semite, then one simply had nothing to do with him. And I recall very few anti–Semitic excesses. Maybe someone did occasionally say "Filthy Yid," but no more than once or twice in my life, at the most. One quite simply led separate lives, also at school.

I knew about anti–Semitism but never spoke about it — neither to my parents nor to my grandfather. Anti-Semitism was a natural phenomenon, and there was no need to talk about it. Just as you might say that sexuality is a natural phenomenon, and I similarly hardly ever discussed sexual matters with my father. This happened very, very rarely, but the comparison is valid — there are things one simply doesn't talk about.

The whole world knew that there would be an Anschluss. Only the Austrian Jews didn't know. They didn't want to know. My grandfather, for instance, could easily have emigrated or, before the Anschluss trouble, gone to Britain or America, as a guest, not as a refugee. But he didn't want to leave Vienna. He felt he was Viennese and didn't want to leave. In point of fact, I didn't suspect that there was any danger. I mean to say, I just lived there as a boy of 17, and I had a wonderful time there as a teenager. I believe that before the Anschluss nobody talked about the Anschluss. But in the end it happened all the same and, yes, we were all greatly surprised.

Sir Ernst Gombrich
London

Sir Ernst Gombrich, OM, CBE, born 1909 in Vienna, attended
schools there until graduation from secondary school. Studied
history of art at the University of Vienna, gaining his doctor-
ate in 1933. Temporary employment at the Warburg Institute,
London, 1936. During the war, worked at the BBC Monitoring
Service. Again at the Warburg Institute, 1945–50; visiting professor at Harvard University, 1950 and 1953; Slade Professor of
Art, Oxford, 1950–53; Director of the Warburg Institute,
1959–76 (during which period, numerous visiting professorships in Europe and the U.S.A.). Author of 15 art history and
theoretical books, translated into over 20 languages. The most
important: *The Story of Art* (1950), *Art and Illusion* (1960), *Norm
and Form* (1966), *The Sense of Order* (1979), *New Light on Old
Masters* (1986). Holder of numerous British and international
honors, including the British Order of Merit, the Austrian Cross
of Honor for Science and Art (first class), the Wittgenstein
Prize, and the Goethe Prize of the City of Frankfurt. Member
of numerous European and American academies.

I was born in 1909. In 1918 I was therefore nine years old; of course,
I well remember both the First World War and the collapse of the monarchy. My father was a respected, but by no means affluent, lawyer. (That he
was respected is proved by the fact that he was vice president of the Dis-
ciplinary Council of Lawyers.) My mother was a piano teacher, really a concert pianist; she had studied with Leschetitzky and belonged to the circle
of Gustav Mahler and other musicians. My parents therefore were educated people. We had a lot of books at home, and music played an important part in our homelife. I had two older sisters, neither of them alive any

25

more. One was a violinist and had been a pupil of Adolf Busch's. Busch was a permanent guest in our house. Music was certainly central to our lives, but so was nature and the visual arts. We lived in Gumpendorfer-strasse, quite close to the Getreidemarkt. On Sundays our father would either go on an outing with us or else take us to the Kunsthistorisches Museum, Vienna's art museum. Thus the most varied spheres of knowledge were really a matter of course for us from the outset.

I was a sickly child, or maybe my parents were rather anxious — at any rate, I went to a private elementary school. In 1920 I was sent to Sweden under a Save the Children program, designed to bring starving children to that country and there fatten them up. This is bound to sound a little odd, if with my present-day bulk I describe myself as a starving child, but it is quite true that of five degrees of undernourishment I was in the fourth. My mother's brother, who was a pediatrician, had refused over a long period to authorize additional foodstuffs for us, invariably arguing, with justification, that others were in even greater need. He was a man of high ethical principles. And my father, too, had refused for a very, very long time to buy anything on the black market or, as the phrase was, "under the counter." So we really were somewhat undernourished. In 1920 I therefore went to Sweden for nine months and was accommodated there, along with my sister, in a family, and in consequence we learned to speak Swedish. Vienna at that time was suffering from shortages — a fact not now realized by everyone. Nowadays that period is thought of as Vienna's golden age. In reality inflation had hit the middle class in particular. Thank God there was a rent freeze for people who hardly had any income left. Salaries were terribly low. I recall a one-day protest strike in the grammar schools because one teacher, it was said, had starved to death. It was probably true, people were terribly badly off. And then there were those unending debates on whether Austria was viable. "Viable" was a term in constant use; the question was whether Austria could survive economically on her own. There was the famous dictum that "Vienna is a hydrocephalus" — two million in Vienna and, I believe, no more than four million in the countryside. The tension between the industrial population and the bourgeoisie in Vienna on the one hand and the rural population on the other was a tragedy. Vienna was Red, socialist, and rural Austria was clerical, and the conflict between the two camps was unbelievably great. The Reds called the peasants clodhoppers, and the rural population despised the urban intelligentsia, which included a lot of Jews.

We were baptized, my parents were already baptized, and I was Protestant. I never bothered very much about these things. Of course I remember the first anti–Semitic posters; völkisch was the term then, I don't think the name National Socialist existed then. I read those posters and I recall a text: "What has become of the caftan Jew? He now sits in the coffeehouse and is a rich man! These are crooks; they arrived here from Poland as poor devils and have robbed us of the clothes on our backs...." The suggestion was that the Jews had all been war profiteers. Of course, there were such phenomena, there's no point in concealing that. There was, for instance, the notorious Bosel. He was one of those skilful and cunning black-marketeers who allegedly came to Vienna quite poor but by then had become so rich as to be proverbial in Vienna: "I haven't got that kind of money. Do you think I am Bosel?" And Bosel, through his machinations, was partly responsible for the collapse of the Postal Savings Bank, when a great, a very great, number of people lost their savings. It is perfectly understandable that people who came from the ghetto and had absolutely nothing were ready to try anything. It used to be said: If they find a button in the street, they think on how it can be turned into money. The result was that the Viennese Jews were anything but pleased at this immigration from the East. They were probably also at times unjust. But there certainly was a strong resentment of the immigrants from Poland; many Jewish jokes tended in that direction. And the Jewish bourgeoisie, who no longer felt Jewish but predominantly consisted of assimilated Jews, likewise harbored a certain resentment against these Jewish immigrants. When my parents were baptized this was largely due to the influence of a highly sophisticated lady, who was a good friend of Gustav Mahler. This was the circle of Siegfried Lipiner. These people were all in favor of assimilation. Assimilation was, in a sense, the natural program. My maternal grandfather had already sent my mother to the Paedagogium, a liberal school without religious instruction. My own schooling began at the private school on Linke Wienzeile. I had Protestant religious instruction. After that I attended the Gymnasium of the Theresianer Akademie.[1]

Next came the University of Vienna, except for one semester in Berlin. By the time I graduated in 1932 the situation had become greatly exacerbated, by then there was a lot more anti–Semitism. There were those notorious outrages at the university, when the Nazis pursued the Jews with steel rods and beat them up. I once witnessed this myself as I was about to enter the Kunsthistorisches Institut. There was a phalanx of Nazis standing there, I tried to pass between them, but they tore my case out of my hand and I ran away. But I was not beaten up, and I even got my case back.

One of my best friends, however, Otto Kurz, was beaten up badly. And when Kurz returned, Julius von Schlosser, my art history professor in a seminar, quoted Schiller at him: "A monument of our period's disgrace." Professor Schlosser could certainly not be suspected of being a rabid Nazi, but the teaching body must be held responsible for a good deal in this connection.

The university itself did not oppose such barbarism. Its extraterritorial status was just what the radical right needed; they employed "marshals" who participated in the outrages of these student organizations. Then there were display cabinets of various associations which the professors had to pass every day. They always displayed pages from the Nazi paper *Der Stürmer*, declaring more or less that the Jews were the most revolting breed of curs. That the professors grandly ignored all this is disgraceful. One day eventually Dollfuss sent in the police, and that was the end of the troubles. And that was greatly to his credit.

My recollections of that period are uneasy, but it never occurred to me that one day Vienna might no longer be the center of my interests. "Uneasy" isn't quite the right word: As soon as I was a little clearer about my origins and about the situation I stuck to an absolute principle — I won't speak to any anti–Semite! I don't wish to be an exception; I don't want him to tell me: "Of course, I don't mean you," in the way Lueger, the mayor of Vienna, handled it. I remember such conversations from the later years of my school days. Of course it was painful to me when I discovered that someone was an anti–Semite — it certainly happened that I encountered people whom I had assumed to be decent, honest people. But I didn't want to have anything to do with them, that was my principle. The whole business, needless to say, did not happen overnight. It happened gradually. In musical circles no one ever asked about a person's origins; naturally there were Jews and non–Jews, and they made music together; that's all there was to it. Hans Weigel's book *One Cannot Talk About It Calmly*— incidentally, I am in it — describes it quite accurately.[2] There was an excellent pianist who was a good friend of my mother's and who had also taught my wife; we heard that he had been seen wearing a swastika and giving the Hitler salute in Mattsee, in the Salzburg region, where many Nazis met at a summer camp. When he came back he was wearing a swastika lapel-pin. My sister, I remember it well, said to him, "Take that thing off!" and he was embarrassed. Such cases did exist and one suddenly made such discoveries. I remember that the viola player of the Busch Quartet, who was of Jewish origin, questioned him one day:

"How can you be a Nazi, surely you know that so many Jews did a lot for you?" And he replied, "There you are: Even I would have got nowhere if the Jews hadn't helped me. There you see the power of the Jews!"

Groups of these people used to walk along the streets, yelling "Germany, awake! Judah perish!" and such like. As I have said, this came about gradually, not at once. It isn't easy to do anything against a mass movement, a mass psychosis. The professors could certainly have shown more backbone, but that the situation might become a danger to people's lives — that I never thought. Absolutely not. Neither in Austria nor in Germany did the middle classes, the bourgeoisie, imagine such a thing. My father didn't want to know about it at all, that there was any danger — on the contrary.

I received my doctor's degree in 1933 and then tried to find a position in Vienna. This proved virtually impossible. There was a great deal of unemployment among intellectuals then, but my Jewish origins certainly also had something to do with it. The matter came to a crisis one day when I was working in the Albertina library and Dr. Benesch, from the Albertina, approached me and suggested that I apply for an unpaid trainee post there. He was very nice, he thought a lot of me, and I was very pleased. It seemed like the first step. On his advice I therefore submitted an application and gave the necessary references. My application was turned down. That was not only a heavy blow, but also the first real proof that things could not go on like this. This happened still under Dollfuss.[3] Benesch was very sorry. Maybe anti–Semitism was not the only reason; you know what Austria is like, and the matter could well have had personal or political motives. I was never a Social Democrat; I have always been nonpolitical — if only because I couldn't stand the mass processions that were then customary.

Following this rejection I worked on a book on the history of caricature with my friend and mentor Ernst Kris, who worked at the Kunsthistorisches Museum, and he said to me, "You've got to leave, you have no prospects here, and things will get worse." He regularly read the *Völkischer Beobachter*.[4] He knew what was happening and told me I must leave Austria. The director of the Warburg Institute at the time, Fritz Saxl, who was Austrian, came to Vienna just then to discuss some specialized issue with Ernst Kris. He was interested in a Renaissance automaton in the Vienna Kunsthistorisches Museum, and Kris was knowledgeable about such things. Saxl arrived and asked Kris if he knew somebody who could help with the publication of Aby Warburg's papers, and Kris recommended me to him. It may perhaps seem paradoxical that the Institute, which had to be relocated to England, should engage an Austrian, but for this task they of course needed someone who had complete mastery of German. Warburg's handwriting was, and is, very difficult to read, and no English person could have managed this. In consequence I got a work permit for it without any ado at all.

Eleasar Weissbrot
Jerusalem

Eleasar Weissbrot, born September 17, 1917, in Kiev, the son of an Austrian prisoner of war and a Russian woman physician. Both parents moved to Vienna in 1921. Attended elementary and modern grammar school in Vienna; passed school exit exam 1935 and immediately afterwards immigrated to Palestine. Study of pure science at Hebrew University; graduated with Scientiae Magister, 1941. University instructor for science within the British Institute of Engineering Technology (1937–1947 in Jerusalem, Cairo, Malta, Beirut, Amman and Damascus). B.Ed. University of Chicago, 1946. Military service in the Israeli War of Liberation 1947-48. From 1949 to 1978, head of Hebrew Tutorial Institute, various visiting professorships abroad. Obtained M.B.A. University of London, 1953. Manager of the Jerusalem Symphony Orchestra, 1980; director general of the Jerusalem Music Centre, 1981; musical director of Israeli festivals, 1982-83; President of Austrian-Israeli Society, Jerusalem, 1978–93 (in this capacity repeatedly leader of delegations to Austria). Visiting professor in Washington, D.C., 1993. Children: Ethan, Nurit, Orna and Judy.

On a visit to Weitersfelden in Upper Austria, in my childhood, in the summer of 1927, I had an eye-opening experience. Weitersfelden is a small village in the Mühlviertel,[5] where for seven years my parents and I spent our summer holidays; it was quite a small place which my mother had chosen on the recommendation of friends. In 1927 we arrived there for the first time. Needless to say, in accordance with regulations we had to report to the gendarmerie as arrivals from Vienna. And, of course, on the registration form there was a question of "religious denomination," which my mother, as was then customary, filled in with *mosaisch*. When our landlord saw this entry he recoiled with surprise and said, "You don't say! You're *Jews*? Surely, that's not possible, I've never come across this before! In that case I'll have to ask the priest first if it's all right to let you have a room." My mother was quite astonished and asked what this had to do with the priest. And the landlord answered, as if it were a matter of course, "You see, we are an entirely Christian neighborhood here, and we have to consult with the priest over this because we've never seen a Jew before and never had a Jew as a guest." So we went to the priest, and he regarded us with great astonishment and asked if we really were Jews. My mother by then was getting a little irritated and wished to know what was so special about our being Jews. And his reaction was the same as that of the landlord: He'd never seen a Jew before. Then followed a regular, though not too protracted, interrogation. "What's your business, then?" "I am a doctor." "Oh really. And what does the young gentleman do?" "I'm a student; I am at grammar school." "And what do you learn?" "This and that." And cheekily I added, "You know, Reverend, I can even quote the Bible in the original language because I also learn Hebrew at school!" He said that's not possible, whereupon I spoke the first five or six sentences of the Hebrew Bible. Clearly this impressed him, because he thereupon told the landlord that everything was in order and he could rent us the room.

We went there every summer for seven years. My father would come along for a few days, then he had to return to Vienna. The landlord was a highly intelligent and also very musical person, and I conversed with him a lot. Much later we came to know one another better, he often called on the services of my mother, and we were real friends. I helped with the harvest, and we were really fully accepted in the village. One day my mother asked him, "Herr Pressler, what was the meaning of that business? Why did you make such a fuss over my entry *mosaisch*?" And he said, "Well, we'd never seen a Jew before. And the priest you spoke to had told our children at school, in religious instruction, that the Jews had horns, that they were something like semihumans. They have horns which they hide under their curly hair, and some of them also have a tail. One had to be careful with them, they were not to be regarded as entirely human!"

This shocked us greatly. Because the priest said so, everybody believed it. But somehow we got over it, because the people were so friendly and we were well looked after there. We came to know their families. We came to know the parents of this peasant who lived in another small village. We helped the parents when there was a lot of work, when some crop had to be brought in. We all shared in the work, and we had wonderful food brought out to us in the fields by the servant girls. It really was a beautiful cooperation and nobody thought of anything else. They rehearsed *Everyman* and they enjoyed it; they did not play the Oberammergau passion plays, but *Everyman* was to their taste and they worked at it. The mayor was called Hecknagl, but the deputy mayor was called Hitler! This Herr Hitler had the only ice machine in the village. If we wanted some ice cream we'd go to Herr Hitler at his tavern. But it made no difference; no one thought of another Hitler.

Many years later I was in Austria with my wife. As we drove along the Danube I saw the signpost "Grein," reminding me of the road which runs from Grein to Königswiesen and Weitersfelden. I told my wife, who had often heard me speak of Weitersfelden and my lovely time there, and she said, "Let's go to Weitersfelden!" That same evening we didn't quite have the courage to drive to Weitersfelden, but made it to Königswiesen by nightfall, had supper at a tavern and stayed at a hotel. That evening the whole village was celebrating — the village football team of Königswiesen had tied Linz, a big city, 1–1, and it was a real village feast. When we were served, and it was good food, I asked the landlord if he knew the neighborhood well. Yes, he said, he sold his sausages all over the place. He was a cooked-meat butcher. He knew Weitersfelden well and was able to tell me where I would meet my boyhood friends. One of them was called Hilde, and I actually looked her up. At first she didn't recognize me, but by the second sentence she knew who I was. She produced some photos from our young days, and a few requisites which somehow she had saved from my parents. She said she always knew that one of us would come back one day. She was really pleased. And there was something else. Her husband had lost an arm. After we'd drunk a few glasses of wine, my wife asked him where he had lost his arm. He said on the day of the invasion of Normandy. This sent a shock through me; I had been there on D-Day. I was in the U.S. Army and in the first wave attacking the front line of the West Wall. And in theory it could have been me who fired that bullet at him. After that we both understood the madness of war better; we were both silent and drank another glass of wine.

Yehuda Brott
Jerusalem

Yehuda Brott, born 1908 as Juda Weissbrot in Tarnopol (Galicia). Flew from advancing Russian troops to Vienna, 1914. Obtained degrees in pharmacology (S.M.) and chemistry (Ph.D.). Chairman of socialist Zionist Haboneh; as head of Youth Aliyah employed at Palestine Office, immigrated to Israel, 1939. Worked in oil industry (Haifa) and metallurgy (Tel Aviv), and from 1950 held leading positions in Israeli chemical industry. Married Klara Reisberg, 1944 (one daughter, born 1951). Changed his name to Yehuda Brott in April 1954; moved to Burma the same year; conducted two years of pioneer work for Burma's chemical industry. Nominated Israeli chief pharmacist, 1954. Moved to Jerusalem. After retirement in 1975, became a member of the board of Gesellschaft Österreich-Israel. Active Freemason and Rotarian. Died suddenly in early summer 1992.

I was born in 1908 in Tarnopol, Galicia, in what was then part of the Austro-Hungarian monarchy. In 1914 we had to flee from the Russians and arrived in Vienna. Beginning in 1919 I attended the Chajes Gymnasium. We learned a lot in that school, for instance Hebrew; it was a very good school. Some time about 1919 there was an essay competition, American style, which meant that the essay did not bear your name, only a number. Our school won the first prize. Just imagine: Those Jews won the first prize with a German language essay. This made the headlines in Vienna. I well remember how proud I was that the essay of a Jewish classmate came out on top.

After that I went to university and studied pharmacy and chemistry simultaneously. Naturally I had to pay tuition, but I don't remember how much. I don't think it was a lot, because I was an Austrian citizen. After graduation as a *Magister* I wanted to find work. But by then Austria was a corporate state and the head of the apothecaries' profession — *nomen est omen* — was called Toifel ("devil"). When I called on him he looked at me — I have a typically Jewish nose — and asked me what I wanted. I told him I'd just made my *Magister* and would like a position. "You want a position? Very well, listen to me, I'm going to tell you something, Herr Kollege! The first to be considered are the sons and daughters of the owners of pharmacies. Then come their uncles, aunts and grandmothers. And then come the rest. And then there's nothing for a long time, and then perhaps it'll be your turn!" Well, I had expected something like that. When I asked when my turn would really come, he said in 1942, maybe — and this was in 1936.

I ought to explain what the corporate state in Austria meant. The different professions had their representatives. This man Toifel had the power to get me a post — needless to say, an unpaid one (a trainee job was absolutely unpaid). I only wanted it because I'd completed my studies. Actually, I hadn't wanted to see him, but my brother had urged me. I was by then a Zionist, and I knew what answers I'd get. Later I did accept an almost unpaid position, at the Medical Colloids Institute on Währingerstrasse 9, in the old Chemical Institute. I was a so-called *Volontär-Assistent* under Professor Pauli. The interesting thing about this professor is the fact that his son was the famous Nobel Prize laureate Pauli, the discoverer of the Pauli Principle. But my professor Pauli had once been called Tacheles. He had had himself baptized. Several times while I was working with him he'd said to me, "Herr Weissbrot, you could get a good post. Have yourself baptized. Look at me — I made a good career!" Whereupon I told him, "Herr Professor, I am a Zionist." "You're a Zionist? A pity."

I said I'd leave. I had no prospects of getting a job in Vienna, either as a pharmacist or as a chemist. For instance, there was an advertisement of the Semperit works. I applied for the job. I told them I was a colloid chemist and had worked with rubber, and I gave them all the information necessary. They replied, "Please come at once! We have a job for you!" I went to Wimpassing and presented myself. The personnel manager looked at me and said, "Sorry, we filled that job last week." I didn't really think I'd get the job. I merely wanted to prove to my brother and my parents that matters were hopeless for me in Austria.

When the Nazis came I was in charge of the Youth Aliyah. I was in the Ballhausplatz when Hitler made his speech there. I simply disregarded orders that I should not go there; I was curious. When I got home I had a crying fit. I wept for hours — yes, for hours. I had a physics professor who was a half–Jew, Professor Mark, who still lives in America. On the first day after the Anschluss he still turned up at the lab with a small swastika. On the second day, no longer. Because he was half–Jewish. He thought that because he and his father had had themselves baptized and because he was a First World War veteran nothing would happen to him; he wanted to be part of it all. There were all sorts of people then, weren't there?

We established something that the postwar world did not want to believe — that the Austrians were worse than the Germans! Why am I saying this? The Germans knew the difference between what was legal and what was not legal. If they were given an order and the law said they could do this or that, then they did it. Not so the Austrians — they didn't need any law. The Austrians acted without any law. Entirely without any law. Shoot them, shoot them; hang them, hang them; enter a shop and take what you want; break into a Jewish shop and plunder it. The Germans acted only when ordered from above. The Viennese went about their filthy actions without instructions, from a deep inner urge. What was the cause of this? Maybe because so many Swobodas, so many Viennese of Czech origin, wanted to be more German than the Germans and prove it by their treatment of the Jews. I believe that such groups were extra-rabid anti–Semites in order to demonstrate that they were good Nazis. These are my personal impressions.

Benno Weiser Varon
Boston

Benno Weiser Varon, born October 4, 1913, as Benno Weiser in Czernowitz, which was then in the Bukowina, part of the Austrian monarchy and now is Cernauçi in Romania. In 1915 his family escaped to Vienna, where Benno attended the Erzherzog Rainer School and the Sperlgymnasium. Took school-leaving exam, 1932; studied medicine beginning the same year. Simultaneously hobby cabaret artist. Had to abandon his studies in 1938, shortly before graduation. Escaped via Holland to Ecuador; enjoyed rapid ascent in career as a journalist. First novel published in Quito in 1941. Following intensive work for the Zionist movement, began a diplomatic career at U.N. Headquarters in New York in 1948. Moved to Israel in 1960, assumed the Hebrew name Varon. Ambassador to the Dominican Republic, Jamaica and Paraguay, where he survived a terrorist attack by the P.L.O. After conclusion of his diplomatic career he moved to Boston, where he has been teaching at Boston University's Institute of Comparative Theology since 1986. Works: *El Mirador del Mundo* [*The World's Balcony*] (Quito, 1941), *Yo era Europeo* [*I Was a European*] (Quito, 1942), *Visitenkarte* [*Calling Card*] (poems; New York, 1956), *Si Yo Fuera Paraguayo* [*If I Am an Honest Paraguayan*] (Asunción, 1972), and *Professions of a Lucky Jew* (New York, 1992).

———————————

When in 1932 I matriculated at the medical college of Vienna University, and a dangerous life began. Pasteur and Marie Curie staked their lives in research — I staked mine on the first day I stepped on academic soil. I was prepared for it. While I had great respect for martyrs, I also felt very uneasy at the thought of following such a career myself. That was why, a year before graduating from school, I had joined a Jewish self-defense group — the Haganah. The Haganah had branches in all faculties, although its principal purpose was the protection of Jewish meetings and Jewish prayer houses, especially on the High Holidays. It was conceived as a special rapid-intervention force. The Haganah therefore was on permanent alert near synagogues and Jewish meetings, ready to intervene. Except it was never given the opportunity. It was never — probably through no fault of its own — where it would have been most useful. A few heretics suspected that the Viennese Haganah existed chiefly to give a few First World War veterans a chance to shout commands and play at war.

We were not taught how to handle weapons. To have been caught by the pro–Nazi Vienna police with a weapon on your person would have meant imprisonment. To have been caught with a weapon at the university would have meant expulsion from your alma mater — if you were a Jew, that is. All the foot drilling, wrestling, jiu-jitsu and boxing I was taught later proved to be totally useless. There was just one piece of advice from my Haganah days that was of some use: I always carried two heavy keys with me. They were on a key ring and were six inches long. Keys were not considered a weapon, and their weight in your hand was reassuring. That I carried my keys with me on my first visit to the university was a matter of course.

It wasn't exactly the best day. The day before, three Nazis had been shot in Simmering by members of the Schutzbund. But I was too naïve to realize that on a day like this it would have been wisest to stay at home. As soon as I entered the main building of the university in order to register I felt acutely uneasy. There was something in the air. Young men in jackboots were standing around in groups, some with dueling scars. I noticed the absence of Jewish faces. Even though I didn't have my father's golden blond hair, I was sufficiently fair and blue-eyed not to be instantly spotted as a Jew. I crossed the entrance hall, descended the stairs and joined the line outside the dean's office. Again I felt like a complete stranger, without anything to connect me to those others, except a rather pretty girl who seemed to know me. She was some 15 places ahead of me in the line and repeatedly turned her head to look at me. Eventually she stepped out of the line and addressed me: "Herr Weiser, may I have a quick word with you?" Somewhat reluctantly I gave up my place in the line. We retreated into a corner and she said, "This is no time for introductions. I know you, though you don't know me. In the line I overheard a few of those fellows, and I don't think it advisable for the two of us to remain here. Would you kindly accompany me to the exit?"

With my throat dry with excitement I said, "With the greatest pleasure. Only I think you might be safer on your own. Surely these people wouldn't insult a young lady!" "Unfortunately, Mr. Weiser, you don't know what I know," she replied. "A couple attracts less attention than an individual. These people recognize us by the fear in our eyes. Two people talking together can avoid their glances more easily. Never mind what you came here for; it can't be that urgent."

I nodded and we walked back together to the hall. My companion, who introduced herself as Lotte Frisch, talked to me with great vivacity. In later years she became a well-known psychiatrist. Her theory about a couple being inconspicuous proved correct. Although now and then I cast a glance at my surroundings, I had good reasons for giving her my undivided attention. Without any haste we made for the exit and were on the ramp outside when howling broke out in the building. We could not make out what was being shouted, but we caught the rhythm. It was a six-syllable slogan that was being chanted again and again. It was exactly ten o'clock. As we got down to the Ringstrasse the first two blood-covered figures were tottering down the ramp. Immediately there came the siren of the ambulance: the Red Cross had evidently surmised what would happen. A horde of uniformed Nazis suddenly poured out of the hall. They occupied the upper part of the ramp and yelled. And now we could make it out: Ven-geance for Sim-me-ring! Ven-geance for Sim-me-ring!

Against Miss Frisch's advice I made for the Anatomical Institute. Registration with the dean's office could wait, but this was the day when one had to register for dissection practice. Besides, the Anatomical Institute was not the same as the university. There, a kind of voluntary segregation had taken place. The left wing of the building was ruled over by Professor Hochstätter, a German national. The right wing, on the other hand, harbored Professor Tandler, a Jew and Social Democrat, and one of the brightest stars of Viennese medicine. He was very popular with liberal, social-democratic and Jewish students. At the Anatomical Institute, therefore, one was not as hopelessly outnumbered as a Jew as one was at the university.

But this was the day "after Simmering." I was just standing in front of the notice board inside the main entrance when in the mezzanine above me a glass door opened and about thirty Nazis rushed out of the Hochstätter wing in their white laboratory overalls, chanting "Vengeance for Simmering!" And at just that moment a solitary Jewish student came out of the other part of the mezzanine, out of Tandler's wing. He was small, wore glasses, and in his hands carried four newly published volumes of Tandler's

Human Anatomy. He was grabbed by the Nazis. He was beaten up, his spectacles broken, and was finally kicked downstairs towards me. No one took any notice of me and I could have walked on. But my hand had clenched on the keys in my pocket. A huge fellow in jackboots, chasing the blood-covered little Jew, picked him up and mercilessly crashed his fist into his face, several times. As he raised his arm once more I just couldn't resist the temptation. Here was a Nazi, all on his own, his back turned towards me and the exit was only a step away. I pulled the giant, whose boots seemed enormous to me, down by his collar and with all the force I could muster smashed the keys into his occiput. Soundlessly he collapsed. I pushed the Jew out of the door and cast one more quick glance behind me. Up in the mezzanine they all stood as if frozen. At that moment another fraternity student came through the door and immediately hurled himself at me. He couldn't have come at a better moment. My keys caught him full force in the middle of his face and he too fell to the ground without having touched me. A moment later I was outside and saw a policeman running toward me. Unlikely that he intended to pin a medal on me. We were no longer on academic territory, and even if he merely wanted to question me, this would have given those inside a chance to drag me back into the building and make mincemeat of me. So I took to my heels. From the left a tram was approaching and, a few yards ahead of it, I jumped over a barrier. There was a grinding of brakes, and while the three wagons covered my escape I ran down a side street, chose the first door and rushed up three floors of an apartment building. I waited for half an hour and then cautiously left my hiding place. After a three-kilometer walk I got back home. I was still shaken, but filled with a sense of triumph. My first day at medical school and the score was two to nil. Man bites dog! I had tangled with a giant — and a mere fifty paces from about fifty Nazis! Douglas Fairbanks used to venture such encounters when he engaged fifteen Frenchmen at a time. But I had not been to the cinema. What use was wrestling, boxing or jiu-jitsu? All you needed was a chunk of iron and good timing. The master bones of the master race cracked like any other bones if treated with iron.

Back home I was in a state of euphoria. I reported to my mother — I had to tell somebody. I should have realized, of course, that she would have no understanding for my heroism. She began to tremble and in retrospect worried about my safety. Did she make me promise never again to take such a risk? I don't remember. Probably not. How could she have? When we were small she used to tell us stories from the Old Testament, really making them come to life. Her favorite story was that of the Mac-cabeans.

The incident earned me the post of leader of the Haganah at the medical school. Admittedly, no one could confirm my story. The student to whose aid I had come had disappeared. And the Haganah board could scarcely approach one of the Nazi students who had witnessed the incident. Nevertheless I owed my appointment not so much to the gullibility of those who chose me: there simply were no other Jews who could offer similar stories, and besides there was no great competition for my post.

I soon realized that the ideal conditions of my first surprise attack could not be readily repeated. On that occasion everything had happened so quickly that there was no time for fear. To enter a tumult at the Physiological Institute or elsewhere with cool intent, moreover as the leader of a handful of brave but nervous young men, was something entirely different. I had to display a calm and collected mien, an air of self-confidence even in the most tricky situations. Our operations were not overly successful: Only rarely did we succeed in "rescuing" Jewish colleagues who were trapped in a lecture theater and beaten up at the end of the lecture. But we fought bravely when we attacked Nazis lurking outside a lecture room. Unfortunately there were also enough Nazis inside, who would start their attacks at the end of the lecture while the professor would grandly look away.

But my keys invariably went into action. There was something like a ritual upon entry to one of the institutes. The Nazis were lined up in a phalanx and we did likewise. At first, verbal abuse was exchanged. My place was always in the front rank. As soon as I noticed one of the Nazis reaching into his pocket I'd strike his face before he got there. I didn't get as much as a scratch even once. And soon we benefited from Austro-fascism when, beginning in February 1934, the police were made responsible for law and order also on academic soil. From then on we were able to concentrate more calmly on our studies. However, three months before I completed my studies Hitler came, and so I never became a doctor. Nevertheless, my Haganah days were to prove very useful for the kind of life that lay in front of me.

Lisa Fittko
Chicago

Lisa Fittko, née Lisa Eckstein. Born August 23, 1909, in Ung-
var (now Uzhgorod, Ukraine). Attended elementary school in
Vienna, Schönbrunner Strasse, followed by Lyzeum des Wiener
Frauenerwerbsvereins on Margaretengürtel. In 1922 her fam-
ily moved to Berlin. Worked as a translator beginning in 1930.
In 1933, sought for anti–Nazi activity, she escaped to Prague.
Married in Prague, 1934. Remained in Prague until the end of
1935, in Basle from then until 1938, and then in Paris until the
outbreak of war, 1939. Internment camp at Gurs, southern
France, then in Marseilles and various locations along the
Franco-Spanish frontier. Until November 1941, together with
her husband, she helped German and Austrian refugees from
Hitler to escape over the Pyrenees; these included the philoso-
pher Walter Benjamin. Immigrated to Cuba in 1941; admitted
to U.S.A. in 1948. Occupations: foreign-language correspondent and administrator at University of Chicago, retired 1974.
Publications: *Mein Weg über die Pyrenäen* [*My Path Across the
Pyrenees*], Munich 1985; *Solidarität unerwünscht: Erinnerungen
1933–40* [*Solidarity Not Wanted: Recollections 1933–40*], Munich
1992.

Vienna is the place of my childhood, and that's something you never
lose. But my activity against and my attitude toward the Nazis — that part
of my life, those experiences, were concentrated on Berlin, where my parents moved when I was 12. Vienna therefore is the city of my childhood,
and hidden behind this is also a large clutch of childhood memories. These
include some very disagreeable memories of anti–Semitism at school, on
the part of the teachers. For instance, I remember my elementary school.
I lived in Margaretenstrasse and across the road from us was a stationer's.

There I discovered small notebooks bound in pink and blue, and the most wonderful thing about them was a little mirror in them. My school was in Schönbrunner Strasse, a rather proletarian neighborhood, whereas Margaretenstrasse was rather middle class. I gave such a little book to my friend, and at once all the other girls at school asked me to get them little books too. I was glad to do so, and just as I'd given them to them the teacher came in. When I got home I asked: "Mummy, what is Jewish mercantile spirit?" That woman actually used the entire German lesson to talk about Jewish mercantile spirit. I don't think the other children understood it either. "Filthy Jews" they understood, but what it meant they didn't. And I didn't know what Jewish mercantile spirit was. Naturally my mother asked who'd said this. But Vienna then wasn't a place where one could protest about that. The whole business happened in 1919, the year after the revolution.

I knew that I was Jewish. But my parents had no Jewish tradition at all. Evidently my family had moved away from Judaism a few generations earlier. But it was explained to me that I was Jewish. Now and again there was the other side of the coin. One day I told my mother that a girl at school had invited me to her birthday party and that I didn't know why, since she was no particular friend of mine. My mother asked what her name was. I still remember her first name, Naomi, and there was probably a Jewish surname. My mother explained to me that those were families who still observed the Jewish tradition and that they could therefore invite only Jewish girls to their birthday parties. *Why* was a little difficult to understand for me, but such things stick in children's memories. That was the other side of anti–Semitism; it helps to understand the atmosphere.

When I was about ten I was sent to Holland. This was after the First World War, and many children then starved to death, or at any rate went hungry. I was sent to Holland and spent a year there. This wasn't strictly planned — our stay was supposed to be limited — but, as was often the case, foster parents fell in love with the children and, well, it's the old story. I had to return home after three months to enable other children to benefit, but these people then made me come back to Holland at their own expense. They sent me to school, and during that year I actually forgot my German. I had a very close friend, as is usual with little girls, and we later returned to Vienna together. Her case was similar to mine, and we made plans for what we'd do together in Vienna. I don't know what happened, but she never got in touch. My parents then tried to get in touch with her, but they received no response. I was terribly unhappy; she had been my best friend. My parents must have talked about it, because what I understood was that the reason could only be that the girl's family was anti–Semitic and she had to break off contact with me. Such things happened a lot.

In our home it was certainly not the case that only Jewish children were welcome. Except when this was evident for some reason or other, we didn't really know as children whether anyone was Jewish or not, and we never asked. I remember that when I was very small I could not remember whether I was Jewish or Christian, and I had to be told repeatedly. "What are we? Jewish or Christian? And which is better?" Whatever we were told was better, that we evidently were. Well, these are childhood memories. I also have positive recollections of, for instance, the Christmas market. We observed Christmas, but not as a religious festival. There was no inclination in my family to change our religion, unlike some uncles and aunts in our wider family. But within our home we were Jewish, but this didn't matter a lot.

Much later, after years of exile in the U.S.A., I felt nostalgic for Vienna. I still had a girlfriend there, not the one from Holland, but one whose friendship I made later, when I was a little older, and I went back there every year. And of course I had relations in Vienna. Yes, we often went to Vienna. I suppose I repressed my nostalgia for the city, because I never talk about it.

When I compare Vienna and Berlin, it seems obvious that there was far less anti–Semitism in Berlin. It was different, there was social anti–Semitism and there were certain higher strata which were anti–Semitic, but the effect was different. As a schoolgirl I never had any conflict based on anti–Semitism. I know that it was the same for my brother. It was simply quite different from Vienna, where a deep-rooted anti–Semitism was always to be expected. Our father, I think, always told us that not all Viennese were like that. But I must say that with regard to the expelled Jewish fellow-citizens there have been omissions during reconstruction after the Second World War. There has been virtually no searching for them. Germany began earlier to concern itself with them and to invite them back, with the political parties and parliament offering restitution and all kinds of things. There, things were talked about and slowly everything came out into the open. Nothing of the kind happened in Austria for many years.

Part II
Anschluss and Escape

Irene Aloni
Tel Aviv

Irene Aloni, born August 19, 1906, in Klattau (now Klatovy), Bohemia (Czech Republic). After her father's death (1907), she moved to Vienna and there attended elementary school, followed by commercial and horticultural colleges. She took her school exit exam in 1924 and earned gardening and teaching degrees at a horticultural college. Served as gardener at Central Cemetery until her dismissal in 1938. Married and escaped to Palestine, 1939. Lived there under exceedingly difficult conditions until about 1950. She continued to work until 1976 and was seriously ill and underwent several operations from 1965 to 1985. Widowed 1965; married a second time in 1979, and again widowed, 1988.

I was a young woman when Hitler came, and I was working as a cemetery gardener in Simmering, at the Central Cemetery. My neighbor was a pensioned head teacher from the 10th District. She was pensioned off because she was a Social Democrat. She was beside herself about how this business had come about and that same evening whispered to me, "I'm ashamed to be German." But I continued going out to work. As happens with tram acquaintances, when you travel the same stretch every day, you get to know some people. There was also a young man who worked for a nearby stonemason. We got talking together, spoke about literature and music, and it emerged that he spoke French. I spoke French quite passably in those days, so it was a pleasure for me, and evidently also for him, that we could talk French together in the tram. Well, and then came the Anschluss. At first one could still travel in the front car, but later they said, "Jews may no longer ride in the first car, only in the second," and so I didn't see him any more. One day I got on the tram and he too was in the second car. "Ah, here you are," I said to him. "Where have you been all this time?"—and at that moment I noticed the illegal swastika in his lapel. He knew that I was Jewish and he also knew where I worked. And then he became embarrassed. As we got off at the same stop he said to me, "Please excuse me, but I can no longer talk to you. You can see that I hold different views from you!" And I said to him, "Yes, I already see everything." This was the end of the story for me, and I continued on my way to my job. For a while I felt miserable about it—this was one of the first injuries I suffered from people.

The decision was inevitable: I had to apply to the Palestine Office for an emigration permit. Each day it became more obvious: I just had to get out, to Palestine. At the Palestine Office I worked as a volunteer for its newspaper and library. There I also came to know the man who became my first husband, who had escaped from Klagenfurt. Klagenfurt, as is well known, was soon declared a "Jew-free city". Like me he was in the "Blue-White" youth movement. He was working in the department for language study. After all, languages were needed for emigration. So I worked on the paper during my spare time, but only a little, because I was still employed at the cemetery. Then came the Kristallnacht, the Night of Broken Glass. I find it difficult to talk about it; it was so horrible. They came along on their motorbikes, and it was a drizzly day. We no longer had a telephone there and next door, at the Jewish Community Office, there wasn't one either; the Nazis had cut it off. We, a widowed colleague and I, were entirely alone and helpless. So they came in and I saw at once that they were carrying canisters. At the first gate of the Central Cemetery everything was wood, especially the ceremonial hall. The fourth gate, the Jewish section, had a building, mainly stone and marble, that had been erected by the Jewish community. The Nazis burst in, into the ceremonial hall, set fire to it with petrol, and it started burning. We had, even before, smelled the smoke that hung in the air, but we didn't know what was happening in the city. Then they approached us and asked: "What shall we do with these bitches?" You can imagine the state we were in; some of our friends had already been deported to Dachau. "Let 'em run!" one of them said, and my colleague and I ran all the way to the Schwarzenbergplatz, a distance of three miles. We could hardly breathe. As soon as I got home I phoned the Palestine Office to get hold of my future husband, but I couldn't get through; there was no connection. Two hours later he phoned me, apparently from a phone booth, and said, "Please don't phone on any account!

We're totally locked into the Palestine Office — I can't tell you any more!" and hung up. However, he came home in the evening and told me what had been going on there.

One day the doorbell rang and my upstairs neighbor came in, though lately she had been rather reserved towards me. And she said, "Irene, surely you're leaving for Palestine?" "Not yet." "Irene, when you do go, I definitely want your flat. I need it urgently!" "You can only have it when I leave!" "Well, we'll see." and she was gone. You can guess what I was thinking. Less than three weeks later the concierge came. Her daughter was with the BDM, the German Girls' League. And now she started: "I want to ask you a question. When will you be leaving for Palestine? Because I need your flat for Mrs. Selinger!" Mrs. Selinger had a three-room flat on the floor above; her husband was a fanatical Nazi who, after the Anschluss, was posted in Germany. The concierge said the large flat was much too big for her now and she wanted a smaller one. I only had two rooms. I told her I'd let her know in good time. Mrs. Selinger was very reserved when I later spoke to her — but wasn't it odd that everybody wanted my flat? Just as if the people were waiting for me to die.

Otherwise I had no contact with anybody. Work, needless to say, ended immediately after the Kristallnacht. Now I was at the Palestine Office every day, and every day I took the Number 67 tram to the opera. And every day I saw on "my" opera a huge banner that read "Jewry is Criminality." This I can't forget to this day. Can you understand this? I was such a lover of music! We often queued up for standing tickets, like all young people. And every day I had to see that banner, and every day I felt sickened by it. I then walked on to Marc-Aurel Street, and then came a day's work, and in the evening, on my way home, I no longer saw that rag, thank God, because it was dark by then.

When I arrived in Palestine, friends first found a room for us; we had no flat and we had no money. We were living near Dieffenbach Square, which was then a circular park with benches. And I walked around it and dared not sit down on those benches because in Vienna the benches had all been marked "Not for Jews." For quite a while I didn't dare sit down; I really don't know why. These things had simply got into me.

Trude Friedler
Buffalo, New York

Trude Friedler, born Gertrude Marx on December 30, 1927, in Vienna's 20th District. Attended grade school 1933–1938; at the beginning of the academic year 1938 transferred to a Juden-schule [Jewish school] and was there until 1941. Called up for compulsory work in March 1941, first at the Siems Estate near Mieste (Stendal District, Germany), then at the Schicht soap manufacturing works in Vienna/Atzgersdorf and the Wiener Holzwerke in Vienna/Simmering. On April 19, 1942, along with her mother, she escaped arrest by the Gestapo. Lived underground from April 1942 until the end of the war. Secretary for the U.S. Army in Linz, 1945–49, for the American Joint Distribution Committee, 1949–51. In 1945 she met Simon Wiesenthal in Linz and has since been one of his voluntary collaborators. Married Moritz Friedler in 1951 and moved to Salzburg. Two daughters (born 1952 and 1954) and one grandchild. Moved to Rio de Janeiro with her family in 1955. Following a return to Vienna and a short stay in 1957, she emigrated to the U.S. For a short time she worked for the United Restoration Organization, a restitution organization. After short stays in Detroit and Memphis she settled in Buffalo in 1965.

I was born in December 1927; at the time of the Anschluss I was therefore ten and a half. In March 1938 I was in a children's home; my mother, who was divorced and had to fend for herself, lived in Floridsdorf. Until the end of the academic year I continued to attend the public grade school. After that we weren't allowed to go to it any longer; we had to go to a Jewish school. In 1939 the boys' home was closed and the boys came to us. In 1940 we were all moved to another children's home, on Böcklinstrasse, where we remained until about September 1941. After that everything was closed down and I joined my mother. Her Floridsdorf apartment had been requisitioned as early as 1938, and she was a subtenant in the 2nd District, at various addresses.

I don't really remember much of how so-called everyday life was coped with — shopping, visits to the doctor, visits to the hairdresser. After all, I was still a child, and these things didn't interest me: I didn't visit the doctor or the hairdresser, and I didn't go out shopping. But I do know that from 1940 we only had Jewish shops. There were those ration cards, food cards with a large red J, also identity cards with a J. In 1940 we had to adopt the names Sarah and Israel. In the Jewish food shops the potatoes were frozen and foodstuffs were impossible. What we were able to buy was very little and of inferior quality. We had hardly any contact with non–Jews after we'd moved to the 2nd District; there were very few non–Jews there. We then lived on Stadtgutgasse. Our neighbors, Catholics, were an old couple with a daughter who were great anti–Semites. One day the Gestapo arrived and took them away. It turned out that one grandfather had been a Jew! Very odd people they were: The women sometimes lifted up their skirts at the back in order to show the Jews their behind. And eventually they were arrested themselves.

Things got worse and worse. The young people disappeared; each day there were fewer of them. And that was even before 1942, when the deportations started. Those who could emigrate did so. One of my girl-friends immigrated to Holland with her uncle. I don't know what happened to her; in fact, I don't know about anybody. In March 1941 two transports went off to Germany for compulsory labor. I was on one of these, which went to the north of Magdeburg, to the Siems Estate, where we had to cut asparagus. We were 50 girls. The other transport also went to northern Germany, to a cannery. They never returned! The parents of those children were arrested in Vienna and sent to Poland. Our group did return, because there was a clever girl among us who told our supervisor — an SS man with children — that one of us had scarlet fever and his children might get infected. So he put us on a train and sent us back to Vienna.

When we got back to the city we had to do factory work. My mother and I were sent to the Georg Schicht works; I was not quite 14 then. All the workers were Jewish women. We had special tram tickets: We were only allowed to use the tram for going to work and back, and from the tram to the Schicht works was quite a step — over a mile. We could not take the bus; we had to walk, and it was winter. We got some pay for our work. From there we were moved to a timber plant, called Wiener Holzwerke. That was in May 1942. By then the deportations had begun. Early in 1942 my mother and I had been picked up and taken to the school in Castellergasse, which was a collecting camp of the SS. "Brunner 1" and "Brunner 2" were in Castellergasse; one of them, Anton, is today in Syria, and "Brunner 2" was Eichmann's ADC [aide de camps]. They were the ones who decided who went where. My father was a non–Jew, but that didn't help me because my parents were divorced. But a friend of my mother's, a lawyer, had a very courageous idea. (He was married to a non–Jewish woman, and, thank God, they both survived the war.) Well, he telephoned and pretended to be my father. He said, "I am told that you have my wife and my daughter at your place. Listen to me: I am an officer of the German Wehrmacht, lieutenant-colonel, and I demand that you release them instantly!" Luckily they believed him. They sent my mother and me back home.

My mother knew a person who was in the Jewish Police. And he warned her in June 1942 that she'd be picked up within the next few days. So we left our apartment (we had a room as subtenants). We just left everything — and we were out in the street. We first went to my grandfather, but he couldn't put me up. His job was to collect the furniture from vacated Jewish flats. He also only had one room, and he was expecting the SS at any moment. What a life that was! I next went to my grandmother; those two were also divorced. She was living with her sister and niece on the outskirts, on Ausstellungsstrasse. They were in the middle of packing because they had been rounded up. So we spent our first night in the Prater parks. This probably wasn't very clever, but we didn't know where to go. I only knew that I was tired and wanted to sleep. My mother asked me if I didn't want to have a ride on the merry-go-round or on the big dipper. But all I wanted was sleep. We spent the whole night in the Prater. For the second night we went back to our apartment and slept there. There was no one there and nobody saw us. We collected a few more things and left.

And from June 1942 until May 1945 we were on the move as "U-boats," moving about underground, illegally. We always had to pay or bribe; nothing was for free. We didn't have any false papers, only our Jewish papers, but nobody knew who we were since neither my mother nor I looked Jewish. My mother knew a man, a non–Jew, who was the bursar on a ship of the Danube Shipping Company, the ship being the *Stadt Wien*. He supported us. He got us food and gave us money. The ship was used

as a troop transport and sailed as far as Hungary and Romania, to
Bucharest, and to Regensburg in Germany. On one occasion we wanted
to get to Hungary illegally. We were hiding in a broom cupboard. But the
ship didn't sail — I don't know why — and so we were stuck in Vienna. We
also had a friend who was in charge of the building of the Jewish community in Seitenstettengasse. He was an installation engineer and had a
shop, which they had confiscated, on Stromstrasse in the 20th District.
His family, the wife and daughter, immigrated to America, and he obtained
the post with the Jewish community mainly because he was an installation engineer. That was only a few steps away from Morzinplatz, from
Gestapo headquarters, and they needed an engineer every few minutes.
He had a small apartment. We stayed there throughout the winter of
1942-43. My mother also had a friend at the Hotel Post on Wollzeile, and
she slept there on the manager's desk. It is almost beyond belief, the places
we slept in. On one occasion I slept together with a child who had diph-
theria, but mercifully I didn't catch it. There were quite a few rather dangerous situations. We would roam about Vienna; I would go to the news
theater on the Graben and spend whole afternoons there, not for pleasure
but in order not to have to be out on the street. After all, there was nowhere
to go. But no one ever stopped me. My mother, on the other hand, was
recognized on one occasion. She had red hair, but had dyed it black. And
once when we were on a tram a man from the Jewish Police came up to
her and said: "I know you! Better get off the tram!"

On another occasion we were trying to board the troop ship to Pas-
sau when there was an air raid. That wasn't particularly pleasant. For one
thing we should by then have been on the ship but couldn't get aboard
unnoticed, and just then came the alarm. The cabin in which we would
have been was all smashed up, and the captain was killed. Towards the end
of 1944, which was a severe winter, the ship was no longer operational. In
winter it remained at Kuchelau, on an arm of the Danube near the Kahlen-
berg. Only we and the friend of my mother were there throughout that
time. In spring we were sometimes on board and sometimes not. In April
Horthy's troops arrived.[1] We were at Höflein on the Danube. There we
were ordered to sail to upper Austria. The SS were on board, a whole unit
of them. I don't know why; perhaps they had run away. I no longer went
into hiding: Officially we were the wife and daughter of the transport manager. So we sailed to upper Austria, somewhere near Linz, and anchored
there. On one occasion I got off the ship and walked up into the forest,
and suddenly I saw American troops with tanks and trucks. I went back

to the ship and told them the Americans were there. The SS on board and the Americans close by! The SS men intended to surrender. I'd learned a little English at school, so I had to interpret. That was the end of it. Hard to say how I felt. It was simply incredible.

Edith Mahler-Schachter
Bromley, Kent

Edith Mahler-Schachter, born 1904 in Vienna. Attended primary school in Meidling, then grammar school (Reform-Real-gymnasium) in Wenzgasse (Hietzing). Took her school exit exam in 1922. Studied medicine, graduating in December 1929, followed by two-year training in dentistry. Spent four years as assistant dentist and after 1935 had her own practice in Theobaldgasse, Vienna 6. Confiscation of her practice by the SA in April; prohibited from practicing in July 1938. Escaped to London on July 7, 1938, where her professional qualifications were not recognized. Worked as assistant nurse in a children's home in Birmingham, later as a nanny. Married in 1939 (three daughters, born 1942, 1945 and 1948). Following admission to one-year dentistry training and passing of requisite examinations, took up first post as school dentist in Kent in January 1941. Became chief dentistry officer of London borough of Lewisham in 1964, with responsibility for school dental care of some 250,000 children. Retired, 1969, followed by work in her husband's practice until 1980. Dr. Mahler-Schachter died in 1995. She was 91.

To explain the question of my name: My grandfather and Gustav Mahler's father were brothers. Hence my father and Gustav Mahler were first cousins. But they never met. My grandmother gave Gustav Mahler his first piano lessons.

I was born in 1904 in Vienna and grew up in a family which was totally agnostic. I never learned anything about religion. But there was a childhood experience which I haven't forgotten to this day. When I started school I was the only child of Jewish extraction in my class. And suddenly all the other children, who had known me very well from the park, no longer wanted to play with me. So I asked one of those children, one I was particularly fond of, "Why won't you play with me any more?" And she answered, "My mother has forbidden me, because you are a piggish Jewish child!" I was six at the time. I was horrified and very unhappy about it. But I didn't say anything to anyone.

There was a teacher at school who realized the situation and felt sorry for me, so she tried to interest me in the Catholic religion and to explain everything to me. Needless to say, I was enthusiastic and fascinated to hear about Jesus and all those other thrilling stories. And then she allowed me to go along to Mass once a week. So I secretly got up early and for several months went to church most enthusiastically and was deeply, oh yes, incredibly deeply, impressed. And one day when we came out of church in double file, my father happened to come out of a door opposite, saw me, grabbed me and boxed my ear. He dragged me home and was terribly angry. Naturally, I couldn't understand what I had done wrong, and I was frightfully unhappy. And this childhood trauma has been with me all my life.

After my five years of studying medicine I spent another two studying dentistry. Then my father bought me a practice. That was in 1937. This had been the practice of a Jewish dentist who had gone to France or England, and he was quite horrified that someone like me was going to run the practice, as he was convinced that there was no future for Jews in Austria. This colleague proved quite right. As for us, we were totally unsuspecting; we probably had our heads in the sand like ostriches. We were always hearing how terrible things were in Germany, in Germany as it was just before Hitler became Reich chancellor, with Brownshirts and SS men standing at every corner, abusing Jews. As I say, we indulged in an ostrich policy: There was the evidence but we didn't want to see it. We knew that young people wearing white socks were Nazis. But since my father had served in the army in World War One and was quite convinced that nothing would happen to him, I didn't really worry too much.

I well remember an experience the day before the Anschluss. I had met my future husband at the university, and we were by then very close and he came home for supper. And I said, "Something terrible is happening, the people outside seem to have gone mad. I believe Hitler is going to march in!" And he said, "Don't talk such nonsense, let's eat!" That was on March 11. So I brought his supper in. Our radio was just then being repaired, but a little later my mother phoned and amid tears gave me the news of the entry of Hitler's troops. And then my girlfriend also rang, asking me to go to her straight away, to Mariahilfer Strasse. My man then really lost his appetite, and we both left the flat. We were living quite close to Mariahilfer Strasse, in a corner building belonging to the Bible Society. And there we saw thousands of people making for Heldenplatz with torches. We were the only ones swimming, as it were, against the tide, close to the walls of the buildings, and it was quite frightening. He got on the nearest tram to go to his mother, and I went to my girlfriend. And the next time I saw my husband — we weren't actually married then — was in July, and that was in England. Within 36 hours he dropped everything and, along with a friend who happened to be in Vienna at the time, took the train. He left Austria without any difficulties. He and his friend, a native Austrian who had been living in Switzerland for many years, then went on to England. His friend had to lend him £60 because we were only allowed to leave Vienna with the equivalent of £2 sterling.

Of course I have bad memories of the period immediately after the Anschluss. For one thing I was horrified at the way everybody was behaving, at the way friends suddenly dropped me. But there were also friends who were incredibly supportive, and this was a time when I could see what people were worth. My father, for instance, had a practice with a cousin in Meidling, and a former technician, who had been dismissed for theft fifteen years earlier, turned up within a week and said, "Get out, this is now my practice!" And they had to get out. I had been living in the building of the Bible Society, and within five days I received a registered letter to the effect that the whole building had to be evacuated because it was to become a residence for the Brownshirts. There were perhaps some forty or fifty apartments in the building — whether they were Jewish or Aryan, I don't know. I had my surgery there. And even before this short period had elapsed they began to break through the dividing walls. I then moved in again with my parents and secretly continued working as a dentist for a colleague. My girlfriend, who now lives here in England, had attended the school in Wenzgasse, the Reform-Realgymnasium. And there the teachers behaved very meanly to Jewish children, expelling them from school even before the law to this effect was passed. They simply acted on their own initiative. They told the principal, "These are Jewish and half–Jewish children, and all Jewish children have to go!"

A curious thing was that a few weeks after the Anschluss, I had a letter from the by-then-Nazified Medical Chamber, saying that as a doctor I was exempt from street-sweeping — which many Jews had to do. A remarkable privilege, wasn't it? I also had another interesting experience. I had a dog and I wanted to find him a new family, a new home. I put an ad in the journal of the Medical Chamber. And I received a letter from somebody: "We'll consider it. Surely you'll be able to tell me if the dog is of Jewish extraction." This is the kind of thing you can't forget. By then all Jews were extremely worried and one had to stand in line for hours in order to get out. My parents weren't worried at all at that time. Of course we had great difficulties getting a visa, but I was helped by a woman friend, a physicist, Professor Berta Karlik, a famous nuclear physicist who died recently. She had contacts with the British Federation of University Women, and although in Vienna I never belonged to the association of women graduates, she gave me her full support. Thus I was one of the first university graduates to escape to England. In Britain there was an International Federation of University Women and there was a refugee committee. They actually flew a person to Vienna in order to get a visa for me.

Erna Zeichner
Tel Aviv

Erna Zeichner, born October 26, 1922, in Klagenfurt. Her father, Moritz Zeichner, was a Carinthian Defense Fighter who had been awarded the Carinthian Cross. Attended elementary and four-year secondary schools in Klagenfurt, followed by training as a nursery nurse at the municipal kindergarten in Klagenfurt. During Klagenfurt's "cleansing" of Jews toward the end of 1938, her family was compelled to move to Vienna after her father had been detained in concentration camps for six months (he returned to Klagenfurt in December). In the early summer of 1939, Erna Zeichner was sent to the agricultural Hachscharach camp — a camp to prepare young Jews for immigration to Palestine — on the Markhof Estate, near Marchegg. Escaped from Austria on an illegal Palestine transport down the Danube in December 1939; along with 1,200 other refugees, she was trapped in Yugoslavia from January 1940 until March 1941. Following receipt of a British immigration permit, arrived in Palestine on April 6, 1941. Married 1946 (two children, nine grandchildren). Worked as a secretary, foreign-language correspondent and, after brief training in 1963, language teacher in the adult education program for German, English, and Hebrew. Enrolled at Hebrew University, receiving her B.A. in 1989. Mother killed in Kielce (Poland), brother in Auschwitz.

I was born in Klagenfurt in 1922. At the time of the Anschluss I was therefore 15½, and I have still-vivid memories of it. The situation was tense, but we didn't think the Germans would march in. Toward the evening of March 12 people gathered in the streets, and there was a lot of noise in Adlergasse. The crowd moved from Adlergasse to Kardinalsplatz, and there was much shouting and cheering. We saw the insignia, huge swastikas, and of course we were terribly shocked. But my brother dragged me from one window to another and said, "Look, over there our lot are coming!" We could hear the noise: There were people coming from Bismarckallee with drums and shouting, and my brother said, "These are our people." By that he meant the Christian Socialists, those loyal to Austria.

My father at that same time was in the same street, at the Adler Café, where he used to go every evening to read all the papers. My father's hearing was bad — a disability from the war. He'd been buried in a pit, and his hearing got worse after that. Nevertheless he participated in the Carinthian defense fighting, and his illness only worsened later. On the evening of March 12 my father suddenly noticed that the café was empty and was told by the waiter that everyone was outside. My father went outside too and went along with the crowd to Kardinalsplatz. He was quite stunned by those swastikas and the people shouting. The pharmacist from the Obelisk pharmacy recognized him, took his elbow and said, "Herr Zeichner, this isn't for you! Come along!" and brought him home. My brother and I were able to go to sleep; we were still young. But in the morning it was terrible. We looked out of the window, across to the fire station and, in the same building, the Bismarck School, and covering the frontage there were those huge red flags with the white circle and the black swastika in it. That was depressing.

My father had been a Defense Fighter, and he'd been decorated. Thus it was easier for him to continue his business, dealing in leather and hides. Even though members of the Defense League didn't actually come and go in our house, I do remember that on October 10 my father would be collected with a band.[2] He was a great man, and he marched smartly along with other great men; it gave him a lot of pleasure. A band would arrive and he'd go down and immediately join the ranks. In other words, he knew where he belonged and he marched with them. That would happen every year on October 10. But nevertheless in June 1938 he was taken to Dachau. The detention order came from Vienna. His comrades from the Defense League did not stand up for him in any way. A plainclothes officer came to the house and said, "Herr Zeichner, come along; we need some information." My father went off with him, quite unsuspecting, and we didn't suspect anything either, but he didn't come back. My mother was most upset and sent me to the police. There was a very big man there, probably an inspector, and I was quite a young girl. What did I want? I said my father had been called away and he hadn't returned yet. He turned his head, looked at the clock and said, "Well, he's been taken across the frontier by now, to Dachau!" From Dachau he was taken to Buchenwald on

November 10.[3] My mother meanwhile sent off one petition after another, with a photograph of the Carinthian Cross, and with a photocopy of a letter from Field Marshal Hülgerth, which unfortunately I can no longer find. She sent those along and my father was thereupon released. It was an old letter from Hülgerth, sent to my father after the defense engagements, an old, very beautiful letter of tribute in his own handwriting. I believe it said in it that the Carinthian Cross was for gallantry, a high decoration. In 1990 I handed this order over to the city of Klagenfurt for an exhibition.

My father eventually came back from Buchenwald, and other Jews also came back, including my uncle after three weeks. My father was able to get to Palestine on an illegal transport in 1939, but without my mother. My own escape was by means of the Youth Aliyah — but in a very roundabout way. It took me three years to get from Klagenfurt to Israel. Of this time I spent 17 months in Yugoslavia as a refugee. When we had to clear out of our home, some Klagenfurt families were most unhappy that my parents had to leave. My mother told me this, because I wasn't present myself. I'd moved to Vienna a few weeks earlier because I'd been told there was a chance for me to register for emigration from Austria. My mother told me that some families — Aryan friends — had come along to the station. She had been telling them, "Don't do this; you'll get into trouble for this," but they had insisted. Unfortunately I cannot recall any of their names. But I must admit that this mitigates my anger, my resentment, of Austria. There were also decent people about. I remember a shoemaker called Pleschonig who had a workshop near Kardinalsplatz. He made shoes for my mother, and when she ordered a pair from Vienna, he delivered them at once and refused to accept the money she'd sent.

So I found myself in Vienna. That was awful, but at least at first there was still some money. A certain Herr Hauenberger now had our house. He didn't have to pay my father anything because my father owed some taxes, and the house had been valued on the low side. But he paid him 3,000 schillings[4] on his own initiative and without my father asking for anything — that has to be said for the sake of accuracy. Nothing was asked of him because there was no prospect of getting any payment for the house. And those 3,000 schillings helped us in Vienna. We lived as subtenants, first with a Jewish family, but then we all had to move out. My father was able to immigrate to Palestine with a transport, and my brother was also at first able to get out. He was initially in Germany in a preparatory camp for Palestine and was then sent to Holland. And from Holland he was taken "back into the Fatherland" — to Auschwitz.

I was accepted into the Youth Aliyah school. Its principal, a Dr. Sonntag, was a wonderful person. I no longer recall what I was taught there: Jewish history, arithmetic — I don't recall. We were there for the whole day, had our lunch there, and in the evening I went home. One had to undergo a medical examination by a commission of doctors, and only the able-bodied children were sent to the Markhof Estate camp near Marchegg. It was discovered that I had something wrong with my arm, and they said, "This child can't work, and we only have a small number of permits." I had known that there would be a problem, so I had meanwhile spoken to an Aryan woman in Klagenfurt and told her that I wanted to work in her garden. She absolutely refused to let me do so without payment, and I said, "I'm not at all qualified. But I can try!" I used to go there a few times a week. Her garden was totally overgrown with weeds, and that was embarrassing to her. A wonderful woman. In spite of this defect — it's difficult for me to lift my hand — I was able to work quite well and vigorously. I was therefore used to working, and I was also a good swimmer. This commission of doctors therefore discussed my case and admitted me to the preparatory camp at the Markhof Estate. Once there I naturally tried hard to work a lot, more than the others. But then things turned very bad. Lists began to arrive of people to be transported to Poland. It no longer made any difference whether one had a bad arm or two healthy arms. So all the children, all the juveniles, were gathered together and sent to Palestine — by illegal transports, of course. The Austrian authorities, the Nazis, knew that these transports were not going to Uruguay. At that time, in December 1939, it was still just a case of "Jews out!" Allegedly Eichmann signed the paper that stated we were going to Uruguay. Uruguay is what it said on the rubber stamp, but he knew that wasn't where we were going.

My mother and I had to go to a collecting point. She was by then living in the 2nd District because Jews were no longer allowed to live outside.[5] Things were very bad in the 2nd District. But there were also other Jews in the building, and they insisted on accompanying me to the collecting point even though it was forbidden to leave the house at night. My mother was very worried about the others, but they came along. And there I remained. It didn't occur to me that I was parting with my mother for good.

In the morning we first boarded a bus and then went on to Bratislava by electric train.[6] In Bratislava there was the *Uranus*, a big ship. But there were so many people there that, even though the ship was very big, there wasn't room for everybody, but we all squeezed up together. We steamed on to Yugoslavia, but then, all of a sudden, it was "Back!" and we had to sail back. It was terrible, people thought that now they'd all be taken to Dachau. But this didn't happen. There were two weeks of negotiations with the Slovaks and we were off again. At the Yugoslav frontier we were transferred from the *Uranus* to three other ships. I was on the *Tsar Niko-lay*. These were excursion steamers, totally unequipped for winter. At the Romanian frontier we were sent back — no papers. So the ships remained in the port of Kladovo. We youngsters didn't worry as much as the adults. We didn't think that things would get even worse. Yet we sat out the whole winter of 1939-40 on board these ships. There were blocks of ice all round; one couldn't get off. Of course, this was an incredible life. I still remember that sometimes my teeth would chatter throughout the night. Even though we were well wrapped up, I was terribly cold. Then someone got me a sheepskin, which was very warm, because my hand was getting ever worse. It was all blue. Later we were also allowed to walk a little outside; that was some relief.

We had a wonderful leader named Teddy Mandel. He was unbelievable. You won't find another person like that anywhere. He also perished. He looked after us, no one asked him to do so, but he felt it to be his duty to keep us together. I belonged to the religious group. He saw to it that we did not arrive sick or otherwise handicapped; we really got to Israel in good condition. In April 1940 we were then brought by tug to Šabac, not far from Belgrade. This was no longer on the Danube but on the Sava. A lot of people got frightfully excited about that. But there was no alternative, we had to go to the town of Šabac by tug. It was terribly hot, almost unbearable, but we survived. There we remained a whole year. The young ones eventually received permits — the rest remained behind and fell into Nazi hands. Altogether 1,057 Jews were simply killed, all our friends. Of 1,200, only 150 arrived — we youngsters. The rest were put to death. That was before the Wannsee Conference.[7] Initially they always killed hostages, as retribution for guerrilla attacks. In what way were Austrian Jewish refugees responsible for that? Then they were all rounded up in one camp and Eichmann signed something. He often got some higher authority to confirm everything, but this one was signed by him. Thereupon all those who were still alive were killed. The men were shot and the women gassed in gas trucks.

We — that is 150 people — were brought out of Šabac in groups by the Youth Aliyah. We were taken by rail right across the Balkans, then through Turkey to Aleppo and Beirut, and from there by bus to Palestine. We arrived in Atlit on April 6, 1941. We stayed for nine days in the collecting camp; the British interrogated every single one of us in case one was a German spy!

Edward and
Edith Arie
London

Edward Arie, born as Eduard Arie on June 16, 1910, in Przemysl, the son of a major in the Imperial Austrian Army. Spent
1914 to 1918 in Sarajevo. In 1918 the family moved to Vienna.
From 1920 to 1924, attended the Döbling Gymnasium, followed
by Handelsakademie [commercial college] up to school exit
examination. Joined the firm of Bunzl & Biach in 1929 and was
quickly promoted. After the Anschluss, forced to help with the
Aryanization of the firm. Arrested on November 10, 1938, and
taken to Dachau. Released on December 23, moved to Prague
on January 29, 1939. Married March 7, 1939; immigrated to
England, March 10, 1939. In the war volunteered for the Home
Guard. Reemployed by Bunzl & Biach British Ltd., advancing
to Managing Director; retired 1976. Died unexpectedly and suddenly on August 26, 1992.

Edith Arie, born August 26, 1919, as Edith Hoffmann in Prague.
Attended the Mädchen-Reformgymnasium there. Met Eduard
Arie on a skiing trip in Obertauern in January 1938. Engagement after the Anschluss. Following Eduard's deportation to
the Dachau concentration camp, repeated journeys to Vienna
in order to intercede. Married on March 7, 1939, and in consequence compulsorily acquired German citizenship which, after
the entry of German troops into Prague on March 14, 1939, prevented her from leaving the country. Escaped to England on
August 17, 1939; until 1944 Montessori kindergarten teacher in
London. Housewife and mother (two children, born 1944 and
1947); many-sided work in charitable organizations.

Edward: I was born in 1910. The first few years of my life really were a gypsy existence as my father was a regular officer and posted at various places. First there was the garrison at Przemysl. When I was ten months old my father was transferred to Sarajevo, and the family moved there and lived there beginning in 1914. Even though I was a little boy, June 28, 1914, remained an unforgettable memory. The fact is I was an "ear witness" to the assassination of the crown prince. All Austrian families had been requested to welcome Archduke Franz Ferdinand, the successor to the throne, by lining the streets through which he would be driven. So I set out with my mother and sister, and we were standing in the street, expecting him — some 200 yards from where Franz Ferdinand was shot dead. We could actually hear the shots, although we didn't see the attack itself. But the day has remained in my memory because it was a terribly exciting day for a small boy — because we were questioned by the police, every one of us — man, woman and child — before being allowed to return home.

My first contact with anti–Semitism was at my primary school in Vienna, where we had to listen to "Jew, Jew, Spit in Your Hat, Tell Your Mum That This Is Good" — the ditty rhymes in German. There were very few Jews in my class at elementary school, so the mocking song was especially hurtful. The fact that I was Jewish was enough to expose me to certain insults. We were very few Jews at elementary school, and we were insulted and sneered at. The teachers, too, behaved less than kindly — and this is putting it very mildly. But it was accepted that in their daily lives Jews would simply have to expect this. It was accepted as an irritation against which nothing could be done, anymore than one could do anything about a birthmark. I cannot remember anyone who thought that anything should be done against it — that is, politically. It was accepted as an inevitable evil: We were simply a minority in a state that was mainly Catholic and anti–Jewish. Certainly the Church played a very major role, doing nothing to remedy this situation. And that had its effect on the teachers. The attitude of the teachers even at the grammar school was often hostile to Jews. I then moved to the Döbling Gymnasium, and there of course the atmosphere was much pleasanter, for there was a considerable percentage of Jewish students, perhaps one-quarter. Later I transferred to the commercial college, and there I didn't experience much anti–Semitism.

Actually, I had a rather enjoyable youth. I had good friends: we were fond of spending weekends by the Danube, we went on excursions, we spent many weekends at Klosterneuburg, we hiked in the Wachau. I also enjoyed Vienna's theaters from an early age. These were beautiful years for me, beautiful years to which I still look back with pleasure. We were all hoping to have a professional career in Austria. Admittedly it was very difficult at that time to find a job. I recall that when I left the commercial college I had countless job interviews, and finding a post was considered a piece of good luck. I finished with very good grades, and the firm of Bunzl & Biach had just then approached the commercial college with the intention of engaging one or two graduates. So my name was put forward and there was an interview which led to my employment in its foreign department. After that my career proceeded really very speedily: After barely twelve months, I was sent on my first business trip, a trip abroad. After that I traveled regularly for the firm to many European countries, and it was in fact an interesting life.

In February 1938, I went on a business trip to the Baltic countries and, on my return journey to Vienna, went through Prague to visit my fiancée. When I arrived in Prague from Warsaw by the night train at six in the morning on March 12, my fiancée welcomed me with the words "How long are you staying?" I said, "I've got to go to Vienna tomorrow morning in order to vote for Schuschnigg,"[8] as I had no idea that the German army had marched into Austria during the night. My fiancée thereupon informed me that there was no Schuschnigg any longer and that there was no point in returning to Austria. But I would not be stopped, and returned to Vienna the following day: I felt that, for one thing, I had to see my family again and, for another, loyalty to the firm demanded that I turn up at the office on Monday.

On my return to Vienna on Sunday, March 13, I immediately noticed that the streets were quite empty, that there was a mass of swastika flags everywhere, that the trams already had swastika pennants, that the police were already wearing swastika armbands, and that, as far as one could see, there was a graveyard atmosphere — probably with the exception of the city center, where, however, I didn't go. During the first few days after the Anschluss there were those familiar enforced tasks for the Jews, like scrubbing the pro–Schuschnigg slogans from the pavement — and my father was among the laborers. On Monday morning I went to the office to resume work. And straightaway I was faced with a very different scene from when I had left two weeks earlier. My colleagues were suddenly totally changed — for the most part they were no longer the people who had been my friends a few weeks earlier and with whom I'd go out for lunch. They suddenly behaved with reserve, not to say hostility. A few of them showed their rejection of me quite clearly and openly. There were very few who wished to show me that nothing had changed. My bosses, of course, were upset by what had happened, and it wasn't long before conditions changed completely within the firm. Soon a temporary head was appointed who was a totally incapable underling and didn't understand anything. Then came an attorney who acted in a much more civilized manner — but the measures he took were exceedingly drastic. The second temporary officeholder was a Dr. Schmidt. I don't remember the name of the first, but he was certainly a lout. He took pleasure in immediately placing himself in the boss' office and demanding a secretary, but he really had no conception of what he was supposed to do. His reign didn't last long, the Party leadership soon took steps to appoint a more competent person.

Bunzl & Biach had about 200 people working at their head office, and some 2,000 were employed in their plants and factories: It was quite a sizeable business. The bosses were six brothers, two of whom were placed under house arrest; they were put under pressure to reveal the firm's foreign accounts and to bring the moneys back to Austria. The son of one of the brothers was sent to Dachau and "shot while trying to escape." In this respect the Nazis behaved like real gangsters. In May two of the brothers emigrated, and during the subsequent months the remaining brothers went either to England or to Switzerland, and only a small portion of the Jewish staff was by then left in the firm. Having removed the top management, the Nazis were obviously interested in running the firm profitably. Those of my bosses who had emigrated already promised to employ me in England, but meanwhile they asked me to hang on in Vienna and help with the Aryanization of the firm, to train the staff, to appoint successors, and so forth. The Nazis had nothing against this, because they were anxious for the business to continue and for people to be trained who would take over later. I enjoyed the privilege, quite unusual for a Jew, of obtaining a passport that allowed for virtually unrestricted entry and exit, as I was expected to continue to undertake foreign trips as before. Thus I traveled to Germany, Poland, Lithuania, Latvia, Hungary, Yugoslavia, and Czechoslovakia.

Toward the end of October, I had just been to Budapest on business — we had a branch there — and got back to Vienna on November 6. And on November 10, I was arrested at the office. Just then, after the notorious Night of Broken Glass, all the Jews left in the firm — there were about eleven, two of them women — were arrested on the premises in the morning and, to the cheering of the staff, taken away on open trucks. We first got to a camp in the Prater, where we were stripped of all our money, wristwatches, and jewelry. But that was the least of it.

Then we were taken to a school where we were kept awake and tormented by the SS guards. The women were not with us.

Edith: My mother was an Austrian. I was living in Prague and I had Czech citizenship. I had been to Vienna several times, alone or with my mother, to visit Edi, my fiancé, the first time with my mother in April 1938. We stayed at the Hotel Astoria, and we were terribly frightened because in the evening there were SS jackboots outside every door. We were in fact accommodated right in the midst of those animals. On later occasions, when I was in Vienna, I'd stay at a small pension in Währing. We then still had many relations in Vienna on my mother's side, whom I visited. But everything by then was very depressing — for instance, one was no longer allowed to sit on the benches in the park. After my fiancé was taken to Dachau, I went to Vienna and stayed with his sister. That wasn't permitted, she should have reported any foreign visitors, but she didn't do so. His sister's children, who were then eight and eleven, didn't know what they could say and what they couldn't. We always crept up the back stairs to her flat on the third floor, furtively, so that no one should see me. But evidently someone did, because a schoolmistress who was living below asked the little girl whether her mother had a visitor. And the child answered that her auntie from Prague was there. We were unable to achieve anything for Edi, though we went to all the authorities trying to get him out. We merely succeeded in being allowed to send him money and parcels. When I was then returning to Prague I was taken from the train at the frontier and interrogated in an unpleasant manner. My maiden name, Hoffmann, provoked the accusation "How dare a Jew have such a German name?" The point was that in a Czech passport there was no mention of a person being a Jew — but they knew. I am convinced that Edi's sister was denounced by that teacher. Anyway, the normal check on passengers in the train was over, and suddenly they made me get off the train. They interrogated me, asking me where I'd been, where I lived — I lied and said I'd visited my uncle. Did I have a fiancé? No. How come? I'm still quite young, why should I already have a fiancé? Despite my terror I suddenly became courageous and answered rather cheekily. I was really lying for my life; all my senses were taut. They examined everything, my whole body and my case, and after three hours they let me go because they couldn't find anything incriminating. Not until I was back on the train and had locked myself in the bathroom did I start howling.

When Edi came out of Dachau in January, his sister wanted me to come to Vienna. But I didn't dare go again. In the end, at my uncle's suggestion, I flew to Vienna. At least I didn't have to pass that frightful frontier at Gmünd. I was let in and out again unmolested. Edi was waiting for me at the downtown office of the airline, and I had the shock of my life. He was mere skin and bones, with his head shaved bald, thin, starved, covered with chilblains — it was horrible. Nevertheless he had to go to the office every day and continue working until eventually he could come to us in Prague. One can never forget these shocking experiences. How he got out of Dachau, we don't know. Whether this Dr. Schmidt, the temporary administrator, had interceded for him, or whether it was because he promised to immigrate to England, or whether they released people because of overcrowding, we just don't know — to us it certainly was like a miracle. Edward's sister went to see that administrator, that Schmidt, and reproached him for having promised that nothing would happen to Edi, which was very brave of her, because when she went there we didn't know if she'd ever come back. You must imagine the strain it was even to talk to those swastika gods. After all, one had no rights whatever; one was at their mercy.

Even before, I had always — whenever he was in Prague — tried to persuade Edi to leave Vienna. But he was determined to hang on. He had promised his firm he would stay, and he wanted to wait for the British visa. This he eventually got in Prague in March. As soon as he had the visa he said, "So now we can get married. Then you can come to England with me!" We were married on March 7, 1939, and on March 10 he left for London to start his work there. One always makes mistakes in one's life, but one doesn't realize them till later. Immediately after our wedding we went to the German Legation — by then there wasn't an Austrian one any longer — to present our marriage certificate and request a new passport for me in my new name. And they said I could have my passport in a week's time. And what happened in a week's time? That was the fourteenth of March, the day Hitler marched into Prague. On my way to the German Legation I saw people weeping in the street because the German troops were moving in. It was very lucky that Edi had left on March 10, because he'd had to sign an undertaking that he would never again step on German soil. He had gone from Prague to London by plane because he was no longer allowed to cross Germany by train. So I got a German passport with a large red *J*, for Jew, and the added name Sarah, which they intended as an affront. And German Jews were forbidden to leave Prague! If I'd still had my Czech passport with my maiden name on it, I could have traveled to England without a visa until April 1.

I received my British visa after exactly ten days. But I couldn't get out for some time yet. I had to hang on in Prague until August 17, and every day was torture. We had to provide such a lot of certificates — police, reputability, tax payment receipts. I can't recall the precise details, but there were altogether 16 different offices where one had to beg for the papers one needed. And these papers were always only valid for four weeks, so if after four weeks one didn't have all the emigration documents, one had to start all over again. Thus I was at the emigration office, where the Gestapo was established. I moved from one office to another and at each counter someone rubber-stamped, and stamped, and stamped. And then I got to the sixteenth window, where a man in black uniform took all these rubber-stamped papers; then he looked at my passport and said: "Your name is Arie? From Vienna? I was at school with that filthy Jew!" Coldly he handed me my papers. He had taken my breath away. I thought, this is the end.

Edward: As I said, I was arrested in November 1938. What did they do with us? Well, it began in that hall in the Prater, where SA men treated us like circus horses. They had whips and we had to run in a circle, do one hundred kneebends, leap frog — they thought up all kinds of games to amuse themselves and to torture us. That went on for hours. And don't forget: I was still young, but there were also old people among us, old men who after a short while dropped like flies and couldn't go on. We were kept busy like that for hours on end, and then we were moved to a school where we spent the night. And there it all continued, they invented similar things to keep us busy. We were lucky if we were left alone for an hour. Fortunately the SA and SS men also got tired. After that they moved us to the Rossau barracks. From there some of the internees, those who already had their emigration fixed up, were discharged. Others, however, were gotten ready for transportation to Dachau. Selection was quite arbitrary. They needed 600 or 1,000 people for the train and they decided quite simply: "You to the left, you to the right, you straight ahead." Thus they met their target for captured detainees.

At about eight in the evening we were taken to the railway by truck and loaded into cattle wagons — 50 to 60 men to a wagon. These, of course, were locked from outside; there were no toilets, nothing to eat, nothing to drink. The journey, with a lot of stops, continued throughout the night and the following day, and after about 24 hours we arrived at Dachau. There we were detrained and we were happy to breathe fresh air again, because you just can't imagine what the air in the cattle car without a toilet was like after 24 hours. Of course we were starved and dehydrated. First we were shaved — our heads, too, were clean-shaven — then we were photographed and forced to wash. Our clothes, even our underclothes, were taken away, and we were given the customary striped concentration-camp uniform. Accommodation was in large wooden hutments or "blocks." There were 30 of these in Dachau. The block guards were prisoners too — mostly political prisoners, Communists, who by then had degenerated into veritable animals. Reveille was at four in the morning: We were given black coffee — or, more accurately, black water — and a piece of bread. At five there was a roll call in the vast barrack-square, and we had to stand at attention from five to eight o'clock. The older people simply collapsed. That was the roll call, and this happened every day. Of course it was the beginning of winter then, and we stood there in our cotton uniforms without underwear. At the end of those three hours we were made to run at the double and again sentenced to various activities; leap frog was a favorite exercise in Dachau. This is how the morning passed. After that we got some kind of fish soup or something watery for lunch. In the afternoon they again thought up some "games" for us.

We were not detailed for any work — for that they had earlier prisoners, political prisoners. They were able to work but we weren't allowed to. In a sense the political prisoners were better off than the Jews in that they could work, which was a better, healthier, life — but there wasn't a lot of difference.

There was a canteen, and if our families sent us money we were able to buy some extras in order to survive. In December, however, real winter temperatures set in and there was a lot of frostbite. Permits for people to be released kept arriving — those were people who'd managed to fix their emigration — but before one was released one had to see the medical officer, and if one had any frostbite or injuries the release was revoked. They didn't want outsiders to know that people were being maltreated at Dachau. It was a miracle that we survived, because you can't imagine what such a routine of torture meant week after week. I received some money once or twice, so I could buy something in the canteen, and I was also allowed to write postcards: "I am well…" In Vienna I had to report to the Gestapo every week, and I had five weeks to arrange my departure. Nevertheless,

I handed over my duties to my successors in the firm during the weeks left to me — January and February 1939.

I wanted my father to come to England with me, but he said, "No, no. What an idea. I don't want to be a burden to the two of you. I have my pension here. As an ex-officer nothing will happen to me. You can rely on that!" He probably wanted to make things easier for me. He was one of many who had served in the same army as Hitler, he had decorations, but none of this made any difference to the Nazis. He was allowed to remain in Vienna until 1942, then he was deported to Terezín and there he died.[9] He starved to death. He was in excellent health, a very fit person, and he died of starvation in April 1944. After the war I got some poems he wrote in Terezín, through a Jewish couple who survived. They had no address, they only wrote, "Edward Arie, Bunzl & Biach, London," but their letter reached me. They sent me what he had left — photographs of us and the family and a very, very sad poem and letters. It was deeply distressing. They told us when he had died. They themselves survived and could report everything to me. Four weeks before his death he had, in his beautiful handwriting, written a poem to me: "Where Are You...?" — a poem that clearly shows how lonely he was there.

Edith: It was not until very much later in England that I learned about my husband's time at Dachau and his tortures. For a very long time he was unable to talk about it — unable and unwilling. It had all been obvious enough, his appearance revealed what he'd been through. It took years before he could bring himself to speak about these experiences. They had actually made him sign a paper at Dachau that he would never speak about his time there or about his experiences; they actually demanded that! And in Austria afterwards they acted as if Dachau had been no big deal. A few years after the war — we were still all of us rather badly off — my husband applied to an Austrian authority for compensation for his maltreatment. Back came a form and a letter which said, "Please submit evidence that you were maltreated at Dachau." Edi was so enraged that he tore up the letter and swore to himself: "Never, never again..."

Stella Rotenberg

Leeds

Stella Rotenberg, born as Stella Sigmann on March 27, 1916, in Vienna. Attended elementary and grammar school, taking her school exit exam in 1936. Studied medicine for two years, compelled to discontinue after the Anschluss. Fled to Leyden, Holland, on March 14, 1939; from May 1, 1939, looked after children in an orphanage. In August 1939 granted entry permit to Britain. Nurse in a mental home. Married a British doctor toward the end of 1939; widowed, 1992. One son, born 1951. Both parents murdered in Sobibor extermination camp. Has written poetry since 1960, first published in 1972 by Olamena publishing house in Israel. Collected works were reedited and published in 1991 as *Scherben sind endlicher Hort* [*Fragments Are Finite Treasures*] (poems; Vienna: Verlag für Gesellschaftskritik). The short story collection *Ungewissen Ursprungs* [*Of Uncertain Origin*] (Vienna: Theodor Kramer Gesellschaft) was published in 1997.

I was born in 1916, and therefore was at secondary school from 1926 to 1934. I had Jewish girlfriends, but also Christian ones. And I have always thought kindly of those Christian friends, though I don't know how they developed later.

Admittedly, one girl at secondary school, whose father was a Nazi, was also a fanatical Nazi, and she permitted herself an incredible amount of anti–Semitic and Nazi propaganda. By then we were about 16 or 17. And except for our Latin mistress, hardly any teacher pulled her up. One day the girl came to school with a blue cornflower, which was then the symbol of the secret Nazis. But the Latin mistress insisted that the girl put the flower away, saying, "In my class I'll have neither red carnations nor blue cornflowers." The girl very cheekily and stubbornly resisted before getting rid of her flower. She certainly caused a lot of trouble and encouraged the others to display hatred.

In a sense I grew up with anti–Semitism: I'd always been aware of it. It existed even at elementary school. At secondary school it became intensified, and then there was tension. There were Social Democrat teachers, Christian Socialist ones, and already secret Nazi teachers. But I must make it clear: No teacher ever did me any harm, not even those whom one knew to be Nazis. I can't complain. They never gave me a low grade or treated me any worse for being Jewish.

Did anti–Semitism hurt me specially? No, not personally. Nor, on the other hand, did I ever experience any special declaration of solidarity. There was one thing that was rather embarrassing, but by then I was more or less grown up. This was shortly before the Hitler era and people said to me, "But you don't look Jewish at all!" It was meant as a compliment but it didn't give me much pleasure. This happened several times. And a young man once told me, "But you are tall and slim." When I protested that this was true of others as well, he said, "No, Jewesses as a rule are short and fat!" And that, too, was a compliment that gave me little joy.

I was never politically engaged in the sense of belonging to a party, but my sympathies were certainly for the left. But I must say that I experienced a certain disillusionment because so many Social Democrats turned Nazis — as a result of February 1934. They were incredibly bitter. I knew some who had been wearing blue shirts — the uniform of the Socialist Workers' Youth. And on the morning of March 12, which was a Saturday, the two youngsters from next door appeared in yellow-brown outfits. They were now SA men, making it clear that they must have had their uniforms and flags ready for some time. They, in a manner of speaking, changed their shirts overnight. There were a lot of people like that, and one could never be quite sure who one was talking to.

I don't find it easy to talk about the Anschluss because this is connected with my mother. But I don't have to talk about her. I can talk about other things. She was maltreated, but I don't wish... There is a poem of mine, entitled "German Night":

> Who's that knocking?
> Why is there knocking in the night?
> I know who it is, therefore — don't open up!
> I'm frightened. My mother gets
> out of her bed.
> Goes to the door

like a blind person. To protect father.
There's hammering on the door. Three men with caps,
visors boldly on the bridge of their noses,
burst in. I try to duck
not to be seen, then I hear mother scream,
I grab one man by his leg —
since then I have that scar in my face.

On Saturday morning it was very cold and very fine and clear. They called it "Hitler weather," just as before World War One there was "Emperor's weather." The streets were crowded. People were quite different, as if aroused. Everyone was excited — joyfully excited and yet somehow anxious. I entered a shop, and there was a man next to me who said, "Why don't you come and have a cup of coffee with me," or something of the kind. I declined with thanks: "No, no, thank you, I am Jewish!" Whereupon he said: "Oh, I can't believe that!" And I said, "But yes, I am Jewish!" Then he looked at me and suddenly I saw that he was frightened — and that on a day when the German troops had not yet entered Vienna. But already he was frightened. So I thought, Good God, this place is a prison already! People were frightened to be seen with a Jew: "racial defilement."[10] Another incident — I don't know whether this was the same day — I was walking down the street where there was a jeweler's shop. People were standing outside. I stopped too and saw two or three men in brown SA uniforms dragging a man outside. He had a bald head and was bleeding. And people just stood there and said nothing and did nothing. Whether they were pleased or not, I can't tell. That was in Wallenstein-strasse in the 20th District, near the Friedensbrücke.

I was in Vienna under Hitler for exactly a year: I left on March 14, 1939. That year I walked about a great deal on my own, quite simply walked, finding myself in spots I didn't even know existed. I studied, I read, sat on benches until they bore signs "Prohibited to Jews." On one occasion I was sitting on a bench on Rossauer Lände with a medical student when two young louts came along, 18 or 19 years old. We weren't wearing any swastikas at a time when everyone was wearing swastikas. So they asked, "You're Jews?" and we said "Yes." They consulted each other and decided that he was a Jew and I wasn't, hence "racial defilement." So they made us go along with them. Which we did. Fortunately there was a police station on Rossauer Lände. They took us there and told the officer what this was all about. And he was evidently a little embarrassed by it all; he didn't like the situation. He then asked my name and where I lived, and

I had the impression that he was a little ashamed. He was not yet used to chicanery. But then one can become used to anything. He apologized, and asked us to sit down and wait — but he didn't have the courage to let us go. The country was dominated by fear. He had to put a call through to the City Hall to confirm that I really was Jewish. Therefore there was no case of racial defilement to answer and he eventually let us go. What would have happened if I had been a so-called Aryan? The police didn't know themselves what constituted the offense of racial defilement, but everyone was afraid. Despite all that jubilation everybody was scared.

My studies, of course, came to an end with the Anschluss. That day my father, my brother and I were at home, while my mother was out getting a few things for our supper. We heard her outside the door, unlocking, entering and sobbing. We all rushed out to the hall, and there she was crying, saying, "Hitler is here; the troops are here!" My father tried to calm her a little. On our big table lay my open anatomy textbook. My brother walked up to it, shut it, and said to me, "You won't need to study anymore!" And that's just how it was. It was the end. I discovered this as I went to the Physiological Institute. At the entrance one was immediately informed that Jewish students weren't welcome. I had seen no notice, no law to that effect. That was during the week after the Anschluss. My reaction and that of all others affected was to apply for a leaving certificate. This confirmed that I had been a student for a certain number of semesters and that there were no charges against me. Was there any protest, at least halfhearted, on the part of those who had been my fellow students? To whom would they have addressed themselves? I believed there was nothing to console me or to give me hope. I knew this was the end, the end of our existence in Austria.

In order to leave Austria as a family, people needed money, money abroad. My mother wanted to leave at all costs. But who would have accepted her, a sick woman? No country would have let her in. But my father thought things wouldn't get too bad. It turned out my mother was right and my father was wrong. But with no help it made no difference who'd been right and who'd been wrong. My brother made his escape as early as 1938. He was in the street in plain daylight, without a swastika, of course, when three men came along — one with a knife — shouting, "You're a Jew!" And my brother just ran away; possibly they wouldn't have done anything to him, but the "Jew chase" was "fun."[11] This happened near the home of a colleague of his. He rushed up to the third floor and knocked at the door. Fortunately there was someone there to let him in. After that he decided not to stay in Vienna any longer. He got out illegally, without any papers. He did have an Austrian passport, but it was no longer valid. I remember that we saw him off at the Westbahnhof, and there was another medical student with him, a man called Walter. The two of them got on the train and said they'd try to get to Switzerland illegally. We had no news of him for a long time. Eventually a letter came from Germany, so we knew he wasn't in Switzerland. Then there was another long interval — and finally a letter from Sweden. He'd tried everywhere — Switzerland, Holland, Belgium, Liechtenstein. He survived and ended up in Sweden. But because he'd emigrated illegally he could no longer get our parents out.

Herbert Anderson
Norwich

Herbert Anderson, born as Herbert Fürst on April 16, 1913, in
Berlin; his parents were Viennese. Attended basic school and
Akademisches Gymnasium in Vienna; passed school exit exam,
1932. Attended College for International Trade and, simultaneously, College of Music from 1932 to 1936, completing his
degrees. Employed by an oil company, working in Istanbul
before being evicted in 1939. Immigrated to Britain with his
parents, worked there on a farm. In the British army from February 1940 to July 1946. Changed his name to Anderson. Married, 1942 (three children); employed in tourist industry from
1946 until pensioning in 1982.

In 1937 I went to Istanbul and started work for what is now Mobil
Oil. I had previously met the boss in Vienna and taken him around Vienna,
and I had to do that in English. He was much impressed by my enthusiasm for Vienna and the history of the city, and offered me the job in Istanbul as an escape from the paternal influence in the firm. I readily accepted
his offer. My first home leave in Vienna was in March 1938. Clearly I'd got
to Vienna at the right moment, and on Friday, March 11, as usual, went
to supper with my uncle. As always, I made my way there on my own and
met my parents and him at his place. He had a charming housekeeper from
Styria named Paula Hasenbüchl.

Schuschnigg had planned the plebiscite for Sunday, March 13. All over
Vienna, leaflets were still scattered about for this plebiscite. And as I was
running across the square Am Hof, a gust of wind swirled up all those
leaflets which had by then become pointless because it was known that
German troops had already marched in. But to me this was kind of

symbolic. There were very few people in the streets. When I arrived at my uncle's, Paula Hasenbüchl was in tears: She was devoutly Catholic and greatly under Church influence. And she knew that the Nazis would probably turn against the Church. My uncle, being the head of the oil cartel office and a bachelor, was able to push off at once — which he did. He went first to Switzerland and then to France. Unfortunately he died in Nice in 1940 of the aftereffects of an operation.

My family was initially left in peace, except that there were two "burglaries" both at my parents' and at my uncle's: Men in Nazi uniforms appeared and demanded family jewelry. My very clever mother must have foreseen that. She had left a small portion of her jewelry in her chest of drawers, and this she handed over, but she had hidden away the more valuable pieces, which she was later able to bring to England. My uncle was robbed of a very fine coin collection. We went to the police the next day and complained. But they said these hadn't been official actions; these had been actions by robbers who'd taken advantage of the situation, a so-called "wild Aryanization." Anyway, that was typical of the time and their ideology.

What annoyed us most was that, when we came to Vienna again in 1949, neither I nor my parents received any assistance in the tracing of these stolen items. Surely the police must have known something about these pillaging expeditions. But they not only made no effort at all, but were also exceedingly unpleasant. Another thing that annoyed me greatly was this: A few years ago I read in *The* [London] *Times* that the Austrian government had collected all the belongings stolen from politically or racially persecuted persons and would either return them or sell them. Thereupon I wrote to the Austrian Embassy in London and told them what I knew — what coins and what pictures were involved, such as two or three engravings by the famous artist Schmutzer, a watercolor by Alt — and these were all in the list. But I was told I didn't have enough documentary evidence, and I didn't achieve anything. The Austrian government simply sequestrated our property. A scandal, isn't it?[12]

After the Anschluss came a time of rumors. The most important rumor was always what country would provide an immigration visa. The whole world sealed itself off against Jewish refugees. That was the period of great unemployment and poverty throughout the world. We knew that we could get a British visa, but friends were making for Panama, for Peru, even for China, for Shanghai. The disposal of our flat was handled by a big forwarding firm called Schenker (the firm exists to this day). This was initiated by my father's firm; you have no idea how popular my father was. He had what today is known as charisma. My grandparents were initially left alone, but their cinema was taken from them straightaway. They owned the Schikaneder cinema, which still exists today, quite a small cinema on Margaretenstrasse. Whenever I am in Vienna I go and look at it, but I don't go in; it hasn't changed. During the Occupation, interestingly enough, it was a Russian propaganda cinema.

Of my mother's three brothers, two were taken to Dachau straightaway. But there must have been some guardian angel watching over my family, because they were released within a few weeks. All three of them had served in World War One, one of them as an army dentist and another on the Italian front. The third one, Oskar, was also in the army. He was an electrician, an engineer. However, they were no longer permitted to work. One of them had worked in the cinema, but this now belonged to an Aryanizer. But they all had some savings, though perhaps not very great ones. The uncles immediately started working on their emigration and, after various difficulties, went to Shanghai in 1939. They were relatively well off. They survived the war there and didn't get back to Austria via England until 1948 or 1949, because they had their business there. The cinema was returned to them after the departure of the Russians.

Many of my friends had been cheated terribly when liquidating or trying to save their belongings. People knew they had to sell because most of the stuff they just couldn't take with them. A few days ago I had a letter from a friend. He sent me a picture of the late pianist Liberace. On the back he had written, "We had a Bösendorfer too, not quite as splendid as Liberace's: In 1938 a neighbor gave us five dollars for it!" That is quite typical: Huge profits were made out of our misery. Perhaps I am too soft, but it is human, and I can put myself in the situation of these profiteers. After all, everything was simply dropping into their laps. No doubt, many of them said, "I'm sorry I can only give you 10 schillings, but you should be glad you can get rid of it at all!" That was what one was told. Furniture could hardly be sold at all. But the worst of it was that the flats were confiscated, that those people simply ignored rent contracts and settled in those flats.

I never had feelings of revenge, because I too have faults. We all have a lot of faults — that's human. For instance, I had a school friend who'd lost his father in World War One. We were close friends. He was very badly off because his mother had to fend for them. My father arranged for him to have a job in his firm. And what did he do? On the first day after the Anschluss he pinned on a huge swastika and said, "Herbert, you've got to understand: We can't talk to each other any longer!" I never blamed him for this. I said I understood. I don't know if he's still alive; I never met him again.

Edith Gersten
Brooklyn, New York

Edith Gersten, born as Edith Arm on January 1, 1929, in Vienna. Three years' elementary school in Vienna, no further schooling after escape to Switzerland. December 1938 to October 1940 in a camp at Diepoldsau, Switzerland. Spent 1940 to 1947 in Sosua, Dominican Republic. Beginning in 1944, worked as secretary with a U.S. airline. Married and immigrated to the U.S., 1947, divorced, 1948. Held various jobs as foreign language secretary in New York, simultaneously attained a university diploma through evening classes. Until recently worked as export agent. One son (born 1970).

My father was picked up by the Gestapo during the Kristallnacht, the Night of Broken Glass. I screamed with terror: The leather coats of the men frightened me. He was taken to a gym hall, along with others, and there they were beaten half-dead. But one of the guards knew him and let him jump out of a toilet window. He came home and immediately departed with a suitcase. After that shock I said to myself, There can be no God. A few days later, together with his brother, he escaped to Switzerland, crossing the frontier near Hohenems. My mother and I had a letter from him that "a girl with yellow hair" in Hohenems would tell us everything else. We actually found her and she explained everything to us. We went to the German customs office and they examined us incredibly thoroughly because they probably thought we wanted to smuggle gold or whatever out of the country. They examined every opening of our bodies, my mother's and mine, and for that we had to strip naked. They didn't remark on the fact that we were wearing two or three layers of clothes; they knew we were leaving the country and this was nothing special. Our overcoats were ordinary material with a herringbone pattern. Then we were told: "We're letting you go, but don't ever come back. If you come back that'll be the end of you"—these were their exact words. And on the Swiss side father was waiting for us. The refugee camp at Diepoldsau, admittedly, was a camp with barbed wire around it and one was locked up, but of course this was nothing compared to what was happening in Austria or Germany. My father had gotten permission from the camp commandant to meet us at the frontier at the customs post.

We stepped into the Swiss customs house and they knew we were coming, they had been informed. They smiled at us and admitted us. There were some 150 people at the Diepoldsau camp; the women were accommodated in an old empty schoolhouse and the men in an empty embroidery works. I still have pictures of the camp.

There we were for 15 months; it was cold and there wasn't always enough food. Not that we went hungry. Even if it was only potatoes and cheese, there was always something to eat. It was not a pleasant place to be, and to me it was rather terrible. But the worst had nothing to do with food or cold. After we'd been there some time the Swiss told my parents — there were only two children at the camp, myself aged 10 and a little boy of five — they would have to hand me over to Swiss foster parents. Unless they did, all three of us would be sent back. That was not very nice of the Swiss; it was a kind of blackmail. I had never been separated from my family. Of course my parents had to agree. I was sent to Buchs to a head postmaster called Gantenbein. The people were probably middle-aged, but to me they were old. Not long before, they had lost a son. Evidently they wanted to have a child and someone had got the idea of having me sent there. This was awful for me: I didn't understand what was happening. There they sent me to school, naturally to a class below my own age. I would have been in a higher class if I hadn't lost schooling time because of the Nazis. But I didn't fit in at all. It was a long way away and there were *Foehn* conditions — something I hadn't encountered before. All I wanted was to get away from these people and go back to the camp. I couldn't talk to the people. Sometimes I would get letters from my mother. There was a girl at school with me, Rosemarie, and I confided in her to some extent. I asked what a train ticket cost and borrowed some money from her. And I actually carried out my plan. The post office was at the station, and I remember clearly how I tiptoed behind a freight train because I knew that the postmaster Gantenbein was sitting inside. On the train I then asked where I had to get off in order to get the bus to Diepoldsau. There was a lady who questioned me why I was traveling on my own, and I told her some story or other. The night before my "escape" I dreamt that my mother was ill. And when I got to the camp, she really was ill. But there was something else the same day. One of my aunts, a sister of my father, had a friend in Vienna, called Sepperl, who'd joined the SS. Not from conviction but because it carried certain advantages with it and he'd be able to help people. So when I got to Diepoldsau, Sepperl, who had a motorbike with a sidecar, was there too. Being with the SS he could come and go where he wished. Both my grandmothers were trapped in Vienna. And they wanted to know how we were. Telephoning was impossible and letters were very rare. So they'd asked Sepperl if he'd ride over to us in Switzerland, and he did. A small piece of globetrotting!

I know this sounds strange, but truth is sometimes stranger than fiction. It was decided that he'd take me back to Buchs at once. My mother promised me that she would try to get me back soon. So I rode back with Sepperl to Buchs in the sidecar. The Gantenbeins hadn't even noticed that I'd been away. I think they were notified that I hadn't been to school that day, and I just told them some story that I'd gone for a walk because I wanted to think, or something like that. But they never knew where I'd been. My parents then told the Swiss authorities, "We want our child back, even at the cost of you sending us back!" So they let me join my parents again, and fortunately they didn't deport us.

Of course, while I was at Diepoldsau I missed my schooling. But I had to be taught somehow. I knew the whole of Goethe's *Faust* by heart. We staged a play; we sang songs. I received instruction in all possible and impossible subjects. There was no schoolmaster among us, but they all became teachers.

There was a young man, who now lives in Los Angeles, who knew the whole of *Faust* by heart, also Schiller's *Glocke*, and he taught me all this. Although I no longer know the whole of *Faust* by heart, I can still recite long chunks of it. Then there was a composer. Somewhere an old piano was discovered and they made up a song for me. Of course I missed my school education, a formal education, totally. And when in later years I made an application in Austria for compensation for my lost school education — the Germans compensated people for that — I was told that I was too young then and that I could have continued my education elsewhere. So I said to the woman official, "You know, there was no school at the camp." But this didn't help. "And later, in the Dominican Republic," I said, "there was no school either, there was absolutely nothing!" And the woman official said, "That's no business of mine!" It was no business of hers; the Jews are no business of the Austrians.

After a year or so someone came from America, a certain Mr. Trohne. He represented an organization called the Dominican Republic Settlement Association, DORSA in short. They collected money in the States and had arranged with the Dominican Republic that the country would allow Jewish refugees in. The figure envisioned was 100,000 — but this was never achieved. We were at most 450 people. Why? The Dominican president then had a very bad reputation, allegedly rightly so. So someone suggested to him that it would help his image if he authorized such a humanitarian project. Besides, this didn't cost him anything; it was land that had belonged to the United Fruit Company, which he'd thrown out of the country, and it was lying fallow. It was hoped that Europeans would bring culture and know-how with them, and that this wouldn't be a bad thing.

We've just recently had a 50th anniversary celebration for the children and grandchildren of the original Sosua lot; altogether some 600 people came from all over the place. The only thing one had to do then was sign an undertaking that one would be a farmer for ten years — or was it seven? You can imagine what a joke that was. Viennese being sent to the country! If I had ever been in the country for a week, on holiday, that was a lot. My father had never been in a rural environment, and now he had to work there. Anyway, one was given a house and ten cows; the money was all on loan, and the credit could be redeemed on very easy terms. Ten cows and enough grazing, plus a house. So we stared at the cows. What happens next? Does one get hold of the tail and pump until somehow the milk comes out? So they explained it to us: Here is the udder, and this is what you do to it — no one had the least idea. But we learned it all. And it wasn't long before we discovered that other people could do this job so long as one paid them. The natives expected very little money and knew what they were doing.

Very soon therefore the refugees were working less in agriculture than in other occupations. No one was forced to stay on his farm, and there was no pressure to keep up with payments. We then set up a school with teachers. Teachers didn't do farm work. And there was a shoemaker, a tailor, an electrician. The school still exists and has a very good reputation. European Jews stayed on at Sosua, and the settlement has not been dissolved. My mother, for instance, is still there.

I had a very good time at Sosua. There were 15 girls, aged from 13 to

30, and there were about 50 boys of "marriageable age." We had dancing lessons, and at first it was a real commune. The boys all lived together in several large barracks, and the married couples had rooms in the barracks. The women cooked communally for everybody and also did the laundry. I also started work then. At age 14 I had something to do, and everybody enjoyed their life. We were happy to be alive. For the first time I celebrated my birthday, on January 1, 1941. As a birthday present I was given a horse with saddle, and long trousers. The horse cost 10 dollars, including the saddle.

An Austrian professor has coined the concept of "expulsion to Paradise"—and this is what it might well be called in my case. The country was like paradise. It is still very beautiful, but not as beautiful as 50 years ago—but, then, what is? But there was enough to eat, even though many things were new to us. Everybody had the opportunity to do something. If anyone had a talent for something in particular, they could develop it there. There was a Mr. Wohlmuth who built a bowling alley by his *finca*, his house. Naturally we all rode there and went bowling, and it was great fun. Not only were we not in a camp, and therefore free, which was the main thing, but we were able to have fun. I believe everyone received $5 pocket money each month for working, and in addition board and lodging were provided free. This was partly on the kibbutz principle. People received their own houses, and they also owned their cows. But the milk was collected from them and processed in a butter and cheese factory. My mother's second husband was the managing director of the dairy, for 25 years. He also came from Vienna and at first had no idea of the work. But one just learned everything. After the war, like me, he went to Wisconsin, where cheese is manufactured, and there learned cheese production. Later a sausage factory was set up too, but that, of course, was not until after the war because the machinery had to be imported. And first of all the people had to develop their *fincas* because with ten cows you can't start slaughtering yet, that takes a while.

As women we were very liberated for the conditions then prevailing. We were young women abruptly freed from parental supervision. Compared to Austrian conditions, we enjoyed an incredible freedom. We could choose our friends ourselves and personally decide on our sexual morals. But I knew right from wrong. I had my first lover at 13. As I've said, there were so many men at Sosua and so few girls, and I was very grown up for my age. At barely 18 I got married in the capital, to a European, with whom I came to the States. And when we had been here a few months, he got another girl pregnant, so our entire marriage lasted six months. I had morals but he didn't. Recently, on that 50th anniversary celebration in Sosua, I met him again, with all my other old friends, and we had a nice chat together. At first I didn't even recognize him. He married that other woman and then left her as well — he didn't know what he wanted.

Giselle Karp
Skokie, Illinois

Giselle Karp, born as Giselle Tiger on October 21, 1908, in Vienna. Attended schools in Vienna; after school exit examination, worked as a secretary. Married the young physician Dr. Georg Karp, 1931, first daughter born 1937. Husband fled to Paris on June 18, 1938; she followed him with the child via Luxembourg in September. After the outbreak of the war she was separated from her interned husband. Escaped from the German troops to Oloron in June 1940.[13] After weeks of searching she found her husband in a camp near Nîmes. They lived "underground" in Marseilles until October 1942; in November 1942 they escaped together across the Pyrenees and traveled on to Lisbon. Arrived in Philadelphia in February 1943. Settled in Chicago. Worked for B'nai B'rith. Now widowed, she has three daughters (Susi, Erica, Sharon).

I don't have any secrets, but I don't find it very easy to talk about my story. Too much pain is connected with it, and this is difficult to explain to others. Pain is my primary sentiment in relation to Austria. What does Austria mean to me? Austria once meant everything to me — home, love of the homeland. I always admired the country and found it wonderful. And then abruptly it all came to a terrible end; this was painful. I've been back a few times, but I didn't find my love for Austria again. I went back to discover if I could find my homeland again. But whenever I looked at its people I remembered their hatred, and before my eyes there was always the way they shouted "Heil Hitler!" and their vindictiveness toward all those who weren't wearing swastikas. I therefore found it impossible to go back and live there, even though something of an Austrian identity is left in me. Austria is a beautiful country. I studied the classics, Grillparzer;

I was so proud of the beautiful language — and then I was no longer able to speak it any more because, while we were in France, one didn't dare speak German in public. One always had to conceal that one was Austrian, because Austria was an enemy country. Suddenly one wasn't at home anywhere, it was terrible. When I'm living here in Chicago or in Florida I still have some contact with Austrian culture; I have friends who are in the same situation and who feel the same as me, and those I meet. If there were an Austrian café or club, that would be nice.

I'll never forget the Anschluss. I don't have to do any recollecting; it's all still there — I just haven't been able to talk about it. I recall that we had a maid and my baby then was twelve months old. And the maid always raised the child's hand and said, "Susi, say Heil Hitler! Susi, say Heil Hitler!" I can't forget that. And when the planes flew over Vienna she lifted the child up to the window and said, "Look there! Say Heil Hitler!" I believe she really had no idea how this horrified us. She always used to say that Jews had horns. She'd been taught that at school in religious instruction. We had to dismiss her in the end because a law was introduced that Jews couldn't have Aryan domestics.

My husband left on his own, for France. I stayed in the house with my baby. The child still needed immunizations; every child had to be immunized. There were all kinds of things I had to get done before I could leave the country. Besides, I still had nowhere to go. For my husband to leave Austria wasn't easy either at first. In March 1938 he managed to get a visa for Cuba — on condition that it was not used for immigration but merely for obtaining a transit visa. With that transit visa he would then be able to remain in France. On June 24 he eventually left Vienna. He first flew to Switzerland and from there continued to France.

Life in Vienna was very difficult under those conditions. My friends could visit me only at night. I had a girlfriend whose husband was a high Nazi officer. She had to hide me from him and visited me in secret. And he, my friend's husband, had been a good friend of ours — that is, until the Anschluss, after which he couldn't be seen with us. What I lived on I no longer know, perhaps on my savings. But did I live? One didn't live, one merely existed. Of course I wanted to get out. I had to go to the Belvedere Castle, and there was a long table with lots of Nazi officials behind it, who treated the people like inquisitors, the people who'd come to get a passport. One had to pay all kinds of taxes and duties and God knows what else, but in the end I had a passport. I sent it to France, to my brother, who'd got to France about the same time as my husband. And with my passport he traveled to Switzerland and there he somehow got hold of a visa — a visa to Luxembourg. Eventually I left everything behind and went to Luxembourg with my baby. But I couldn't enter the country because my visa had expired the very day before my arrival. So I had to go back to Germany, to Trier, and try to obtain a new visa. Because of my belated arrival my brother traveled to Switzerland a second time in order to extend the visa. Then he went to Luxembourg in person and I was allowed in. I lodged in a small pension with my baby. The people were very nice, very helpful. I then crossed the frontier into France on foot, illegally. The people who lived in that frontier village could cross there and back, and if one was dressed like them it was easy enough to walk past the gendarmerie post — and thus I came to France.

We next lived in France for several years. It was interesting that people would come to my husband to be treated, even though officially he wasn't allowed to work. One day he somehow left his medical bag behind after a house call. Shortly afterwards we saw, from the window, a police officer approaching our place and were rather alarmed. But, no — he was just bringing my husband's bag back. Officially he wasn't permitted to work, but a great many people preferred to see a Viennese doctor.

The first time I saw the French army its tanks were moving down the main street and kept breaking down. One tank broke down with engine trouble, and then another — and then I knew that they wouldn't be able to wage war against Germany. We were then living in a suburb of Paris, some 13 miles to the southeast. Of course we had to black out and stick tape on our windows. Then we were evacuated — evacuated in the sense that we were told we had to leave, this was an operational zone and everybody had to leave, not just the Jews. We had to leave, but we weren't told where to go. We were summoned to the police and we were told we had to move. My husband had already gone. All Jewish men were taken to a camp in Melun. I with my child took the bus into Paris, where I had a woman friend. She accompanied me to the Gare de Lyon and waited there with me. But there were no trains. We slept on the floor and then, because there were still no trains, we spent a night at a school. At last a train came and we crowded onto it. We moved off and still didn't know where we were going. The adults all had gas masks, but there were none for the children. So I chucked mine away: I didn't need a gas mask if my child had none. We were on that train for days, for several days. Eventually we arrived somewhere near Biarritz. The Red Cross took care of all of us, gave us food, and found places for us to sleep. This was with private families where they had spare rooms. After all, the men had all joined up, so many houses had a few spare beds. There I remained for a few months.

After the capitulation of the French army, my friend wanted to return. There were some curious appeals. In late 1940, I believe, there was an appeal to all Parisians to return to their city to ensure that life became normal again. My friend obeyed this appeal. I had advised her against returning, but in vain. She was taken to a notorious camp and later murdered.[14] She was Austrian too, but she had French citizenship. It made no difference: "A Jew is a Jew," they said.

I didn't know where my husband was. But wherever we got to we put up a notice at the *mairie* or elsewhere, and made inquiries. Lots of people came past, there was such confusion, people got separated from their children. Children lost their mothers — it was a terrible time. There were notices pinned up everywhere: "Father missing," "Sister missing," and so on. We moved from one place to another, and everywhere I stuck a cry for help to the walls. And one day I had an answer: "We saw Dr. Karp at such and such a camp." He'd been put in a military camp of the foreign legion. But I couldn't find out its location — only that it was near Nîmes. At that time I was at Oloron, on the Pyrenees frontier. I went to the stationmaster and asked him how I could get to Nîmes. You've got to realize, at that time and without papers this was a crazy idea. But he was a very nice person. He told me, "All the trains are full of military. We never know precisely where a train is going or when a train will arrive. But I'll see if I can do something. Come round every evening." And one evening it worked: I went to Nîmes by train. First I had to find the camp, and it was so well hidden in the mountains that it just couldn't be found. I had to make friends with someone working for the authorities. No one among the public knew where the camp was. But I managed to find it. And I also found other, very famous, people there. The writer Lion Feuchtwanger, for instance, was there, and I also met his wife, who'd been looking for him.

I got my husband out. He was very sick. Everybody there was sick. All they had to eat was beans and beans and beans. They'd put him in a *marabout*, those were the very low tents of the foreign legionnaires which they'd put up everywhere. The camp had no water. Once a week a water wagon came up there with a little water — for washing *and* for drinking. It was frightful. Everyone was sick there. I obtained permission to take my husband to a doctor in Nîmes. So we went down to Nîmes and didn't return. But all his papers had been left behind and we couldn't get replacements, and it was then very dangerous to travel anywhere without papers.

I don't know what we'd intended to do. No one had any plans. After all, one didn't know what the next day would bring. We needed a room. The hotels were all full; there was no room anywhere. We walked up and down, he on one side of the street and I on the other. We rang doorbells and asked if anyone had a room or an apartment where we might spend a few nights. There was a young lady in the street in front of us, and I addressed her and told her we needed a room. "Oh yes, I've got room. My husband is a prisoner of war in Austria. My daughter is in the other part of France, and I can't go and see her. I am all alone here. My house is your house." This was an enormous stroke of luck for us. We stayed there for some time. She was very, very nice to us. She was a teacher and also had good relations with the police. One day someone she knew there told her that a new concentration camp was planned and that men and women would be interned separately, and not even in the same town. So she was able to warn us. We went to see that policeman, and he issued us papers to enable us to travel to Marseilles — but not back. This didn't matter: everyone simply wanted to get somewhere, farther away from the Germans. We thought we'd be safer in Marseilles; there was an American consulate there. As a Viennese I had applied for an American visa immediately after the Anschluss, and had actually got it. But my husband was born in Hermannstadt, now Sibiu, in what today is Romania, so there was a separate quota for Romania, and he'd have to wait for a few years. But I didn't want to leave without him.

So we went to Marseilles. But my husband had no papers and it wasn't easy to get from the railway station into the city. Along both sides of the platform stood the ladies who asked everyone for their papers. When our turn came, my husband folded his papers as if he'd already shown them to one of the others. So we luckily cheated our way through. Next, it was very difficult to get a room. We found one eventually in a district inhabited by Algerians. The streets were so narrow you could see into the flats opposite and hear every word that was said. It wasn't the best neighborhood. Soon we were hearing our child repeat certain rude words that were heard everywhere. And the night life! Once we heard someone call, "Mother, now he wants it with you!" You can imagine what was going on there. Later we found an apartment in a hotel. As for the papers, we wrote to various people who were still in the camp, asking them to intervene and discover if there was any way for my husband to recover his papers. One day they sent them to him; we'd hardly dared hope we would succeed. After that we waited. My husband worked for a committee that was dealing with refugees, treating many sick children there, and this provided a living. This committee consisted of three organizations, one of which was a church one. One of my sisters who was already in America had tried to obtain visas for us. She had sent them to the consulate in Marseilles, but we were invariably turned down and didn't know why. Finally we discovered the reason. All applicants were advised that it was more promising to get affidavits from blood relations: The name should be the same. My brother, who by then was in Chicago, had sent letters to all possible people he'd found in the telephone directory under "Karp." In these letters he had explained our situation and asked them if they would give us an affidavit. But one of the recipients took the letter to the FBI. The FBI suspected us of possibly being spies, and that was why the visa kept being denied us in Marseilles. We really were very desperate. So my sister wrote to President Roosevelt, and the president sent a telegram to Marseilles. She was invited to Washington and was questioned by a White House official. The president then intervened for us and we received our visa.

Then there was more waiting because the committee wanted 50 children, whose parents had been deported, to travel with us. We waited for these children, although we already had our visa; we wanted to take the children to Portugal with us. In Portugal the Quakers had chartered a ship for those children. But while we were waiting the Germans marched into Marseilles. The American consulate was closed and the windows were shuttered, so we were no longer able to collect the visas for the children. There was no point in waiting any longer. The French lady in whose house we were living came from the Spanish frontier. She gave us an address near the frontier. It was a monastery which had been recommended to us as a shelter. But the priest there told us the Germans were already at the frontier and crossing was no longer possible. We should be prepared to set out on foot across the mountains. This we did with the help of a resistance group which channeled political refugees and shot-down airmen right across France and across the Pyreñees. They were not too delighted at having a small child with them, because they were afraid she would give us away. There were also a few frightful people among that lot — a few who, I believe, would have liked to kill us in order to move more quickly. There were perhaps ten of us, and there was one who had a spare pair of shoes hanging over his shoulder. I had no suitable footwear — after all, I didn't know I would have to climb. Mine had high heels, quite unsuitable for the rocky terrain. So we asked this man if he would lend us those shoes. I think he was a Belgian, a pilot. He didn't give me the shoes, so I walked barefoot. But we did cross the mountains with them. We always climbed during the night and spent the day hidden in some cave. We were caught by a Spanish military patrol, but the airmen made good their escape. The Spaniards wanted to know from us where the men had gone to, but we pretended not to know anything. What men? we asked; we're on our own. The Spaniards were very nice and tried to help us across the frontier. On the sector where they arrested us they would normally send people back, and we were very worried they'd do that to us. I think these people were fond of children, and it's quite possible that little Susi saved our lives. Not only did they let us continue, but they actually helped us. They walked with us to the railroad station with fixed bayonets and put us on a train. They gave some food to the child, because we'd been on our way in the mountains for many nights without any food. The little girl looked like a gypsy child.

So we got into Spain and had to pay a small fine for entering the country illegally — that was it, literally. Well, nothing worse should ever happen to us, we thought to ourselves. The people even got rail tickets for us to Portugal. Once in Portugal we could get away because we had visas for America. We just didn't have transit visas. In Portugal we then had to face the people who'd waited for us to bring those 50 children — we felt terrible about that. But how could one bring 50 children over the mountains? Other children maybe had managed to get out somehow or other, but these children certainly never got out and lost their lives.

Peter Heller
Buffalo, New York

Peter Heller, born January 11, 1920, in Vienna, son of the Vienna confectionary manufacturer Heller. Attended private school in Wattmanngasse (Hietzing) and Realgymnasium 14 (Diefenbachgasse) until March 1938. Graduated June 1938 at the Sperlgymnasium. Escaped to England in summer 1938; at first worked in a confectionary factory there. Started studies at Cambridge in October 1939; after April 1940, interned on the Isle of Man; after a few weeks, deported to Canada. Conditional release from Sherbrooke camp in autumn 1941; studied music at McGill University, Canada; beginning in 1944, in the U.S., studied German and Comparative Literature at Columbia University, New York (Ph.D. 1951). After 1945 fulfilled teaching contract for German (Rutgers University, New York City College); 1945, served as professor of German studies at Amherst, Massachusetts; 1948, SUNY Buffalo. Received several Fulbright visiting professorships to Europe. Married, with five children. Retired, 1992; died, 1998. Publications (selection): *Problems of Civilization* (1978), *A Child Analysis with Anna Freud* (1990). Poetry: *Menschentiere* [*Human Animals*] (1975), *Emigrantenlitaneien* [*Émigré Litanies*] (1978).

———————

I well remember our preparations for departure some time before the Anschluss. When things were beginning to be tricky, my father one day asked whether we hadn't better immigrate to Czechoslovakia. Prague then was still a possibility. My parents were pretty closely following that business with the Nazis because they were left-wing liberals. My father was a bit of a contradiction — he was a left-wing liberal, indeed almost a radical left industrialist, a strange, somehow divided, personality — but that's another chapter. He was always living in that sense of danger. Our apartment was not confiscated, but he was taken away for lavatory cleaning and suchlike. But because he was one of the proprietors he was always needed to run the business. Then we spent hours and days sitting at the British consulate, and eventually we got the visa. My cousin and I got out as early as summer 1938. I still sometimes met my girlfriend, who was not Jewish; but we decided that it was too dangerous to be seen walking out together, so we mostly met at night to go for walks, or not for walks. But that, too, became too dangerous. A friend who after the Anschluss annoyed me by being the first to say "Heil Hitler" to me, afterwards phoned me and said, "You're lucky; you can get away! We'll soon have a war here!" I thought this impertinent at the time, but he wasn't so wrong. Some of my class-mates who were enthusiastic Nazis volunteered for the Wehrmacht and were killed in action. Before leaving I went to a lot of parties, with other teenagers; I tiptoed down the streets and always looked out for SA men. It was almost a kind of a game.

And then I thought, you're now leaving your native country, so you'd better have good luck at everything. So I went up the Küniglberg and expected to have some kind of profound experience.[15] I was so literary-minded and super-conscious, even as a boy I was precocious and tending to reflection and dramatization of my existence. And I had to discover that I didn't feel anything at all. I thought, surely you ought to feel very sad at this moment. But I wasn't. And I probably denied this to myself.

I was having breakfast in Salzburg with my cousin, who was a few years younger than me, and I acted so nonchalantly that we nearly missed our train. We ran after it and jumped on — because from sheer stupidity I pretended that this wasn't anything special and I was an experienced globetrotter. A nice guard opened the door for us. We were on the train and in the compartment where our only case was sitting — the only pos-sessions we had. The French frontier crossing was very unpleasant. One of the SS men happened to be from our school, and he threatened to send us to a concentration camp because my cousin had a book by Traven. I intervened and said, "Look, surely the book's not worth quarreling about." As a punishment we had to wash the floor of the station building. They said, "You filthy Jews made this place dirty with your filthy luggage, so you can now clean it up!" Then they said, "Just as you came to this coun-try with your bundles" — referring to trading Jews — "so you can now run across the frontier!" So we crossed the frontier on foot, to the train that was waiting on the other side. It wasn't far to go — a platform with a bar-rier, just a little way which we had to go. But I've never forgotten it.

Anyway, I first went to Paris, to my mother, and we stayed there for a few days. Alfred Polgar was there too, who was a friend of my mother. He complained terribly about everything, which I found comical. You couldn't get a decent midday meal in Paris; clearly he wasn't happy there. So we spent a few days in Paris. The mood was very depressed. Then I came to England, and that was a big change for me, from wealth to poverty, not exactly terrible poverty, but poverty all the same. To begin with we were somewhat disoriented and lived in a small apartment. My father, who'd had his confectionary factory taken from him, was keeping me. He'd found a job with an English confectionary firm, Barker & Thompson, and he also had some money abroad, but not very much compared to what he was used to. After all, for Austrian conditions he'd been a rich man. I continued with my piano and tried to take an exam with the Academy of Music, but I failed because I didn't know any theory. At first I was to have taken up a job in the confectionary factory of a friend, a certain Jones, to learn the business from the bottom up. But I really took this as a bad joke and did nothing but talk nonsense with the men and women workers, telling them jokes and pretending to be stupid. I didn't want any of this, and I was soon declared hopeless. In 1940 I was admitted to Cambridge, but I had no sooner embarked on my studies than I was interned.

First of all we faced a so-called "tribunal," a group of judges, to be classified. Some were labeled "refugees from Nazi oppression," that was the best category. But others got worse grades because they were left-wing. Proximity to Marxism evidently didn't suit an English judge, and so these people were labeled "enemy aliens." This happened. I was classified as a "refugee from Nazi oppression," but when I finally got to Cambridge, where I had matriculated, all refugees in the coastal regions were being picked up — in a very pleasant manner, actually; one didn't even know one had been rounded up, they were so pleasant. However, we were then put behind barbed wire, and later into camps on the Isle of Man, where we had very little to eat. Otherwise it wasn't too bad, but we were very hungry. Next we young men were shipped across the ocean without having been told where.

One day we found ourselves sailing up a big river, and people said this was the St. Lawrence River in Canada. Others were taken to Australia. A few thousand people, perhaps five thousand of us, went to Canada, and some two or three thousand to Australia. Yes, this was upsetting because our "friends" now interned us as enemy aliens. Also, the way we were received in Canada — at first with great respect because we had been announced as prisoners of war, and afterwards with no respect at all. Strangely enough we Jews elected Count Friedrich von Hohenzollern — who wished to be known simply as "Lingen" in the camp and was addressed as such — to be our first camp spokesman, which was rather funny as his uncle, Wilhelm II, in Holland had just congratulated the Führer on his great victory over France. Not of course that Lingen was a Nazi, but it seemed a rather odd choice nevertheless. Admittedly, he was also related to the English royal house, which was thought to be an advantage. And, besides, he was a splendid person; he always wore rubber boots and cleaned the lavatories and everything else. He always dressed to the nines and was very friendly. He had a kind of entourage around him, the rubber boots became the fashion, and all the best people in the camp wore them and cleaned the lavatories — they were a kind of elite. The British were very angry with us and shouted a lot; one of them hit me a few times with a cane. They were very unfriendly. The Canadians, moreover, were extremely anti–Semitic: "Your name is Cohn? What, a Yid? Hey, Yid, want a bargain?" That kind of tone. Some people said, "But they're only joking; they don't mean it," but it certainly was very shaming and humiliating.

All in all I was interned for about eighteen months. After that they released us in Canada. You had to find a sponsor, someone who'd guarantee that you wouldn't become a burden for the Canadian government. So I was able to study. Or alternatively I might have reported for being returned to England to join the Pioneer Corps, admittedly without weapons. Several people did just that, and a friend of mine, Vicky Rosenfeld, later actually became an officer. I was allowed to study in Canada, the only condition being that I reported to the police every month. Which is what I did. With a bit of a conscience because I felt that others were in the war and losing their lives in a matter that, God knows, was close to us. And what was *I* doing for it? Although, on the other hand, one was rather disillusioned by the treatment one had received in the camp. Some people were being sent from one camp to another; some had already been in a concentration camp in Germany, then they managed to get out and fled to France. And at the outbreak of war, no sooner had they escaped from the Nazis and got from France to Britain without a penny in their pockets than they were put in the Kitchener Camp and from there sent to an internment camp on the Isle of Man, and then on from the Isle of Man. Some of them were in very poor shape from all this. I wasn't afraid because, in a sense, I had suppressed all that. Nor was I afraid when, in the hulk of a ship without escort, I was sailing in U-boat–infested waters. To me it was all an adventure and I never felt the least fear.

The German soldiers on the ship were saying to us, "This ship won't even get there, because by then Hitler will long have been in England, and then we'll be very well off and your lot very badly!" The point was that we were interned jointly with German troops. Later there were also rumors that we would be exchanged for British prisoners of war and would all be sent to Lublin, where, if we were lucky, we'd do forced labor or, alternatively, be shot. There certainly was an odd atmosphere. Besides, one was told that Germany was now conquering this and Germany was next conquering that. Some believed that the Germans were simply much better than all the rest, even though they had themselves been persecuted by them: Jews from the Reich, some of whom had been in the Spanish Civil War. It was an emotionally charged atmosphere, with people divided into political groups, from the national Jews, who only mixed with other national Jews, to the Orthodox Jews, who observed their dietary rules, down to Putzi Hanfstengl, who was an old Nazi but no longer enjoyed Hitler's favor. And then there were the Communists and the liberals.

I can't say that my Viennese home has become strange to me, but neither is it familiar. It's a strange thing, one has all kinds of emotions. Sometimes I came back and felt a total stranger. This was shortly after the war, when Vienna was still partitioned and devastated. Not much later I returned again, and this time I felt thoroughly at home and also had a very strong relationship with a former girlfriend from school. It fluctuated a good deal, time and again. One feels very close and one also feels very estranged, and one doesn't quite get rid of one's feelings. If it is someone from one's own generation one tells oneself, Well, he probably was a big Nazi, he'd have done you in — that kind of thing. At the same time I got on very well with schoolmates in Vienna, including one who'd been such a great Nazi. I mean: These people were enthusiastic. Some were genuinely enthusiastic, they were not just opportunists. They believed they were doing the right thing. It is not as if we were the good guys and they the bad ones. But even so, the thing is quite traumatic. You don't handle it easily.

I no longer have my youthful inclination toward Marxism, because I regard a lot of it as wrong. Not so much what concerns the criticism of capitalism, but the views Karl Marx had on the shaping of society. Anyway, I am not very left-wing, and altogether I'm not very political; generally I am more of a liberal. If I have to belong somewhere, then I wouldn't mind being in the liberal camp. At home, in the sense of feeling 100 percent American, I certainly am not. Nor do I have a strong bond with the Jewish religion. I never had much sympathy with Israeli Zionism, and I have none for Israeli nationalism — on the contrary, I dislike it intensely. I think I probably don't feel at home anywhere.

PART III

War and Exile

Anton Walter Freud

In October 1941, after I'd been interned in Australia for more than a year, we arrived in Liverpool. But many of us remained in Australia and started a new life there. After landing, one was interviewed and asked what one wanted to do. I immediately volunteered for the army, signed some paper, and there I was in the army. Next they sent me to London on leave for a few weeks. My father had been interned for only a short time and had long since been released, and so we were reunited. Thus I was actually in the British army: All Austrians were then assigned to the Alien Pioneer Corps. I had the conspicuous name of Freud, but as we were not being sent to the front, there was no danger of being taken prisoner. Although it was called the Pioneer Corps, it was not the same as the pioneers in the German army; we were a labor unit. For instance, we built small hutments for the Americans, laid mines along the coast against an invasion — it was heavy duty. After a while the British authorities discovered that we really weren't Nazis.

We were then accepted into the normal army. I was sent to the S.O.E., the Special Operations Executive. Toward the end of the war I was dropped by parachute into Styria. That was the end of March 1945, and there was still snow on the ground. We'd been in Italy and had flown from Siena airport north over the Alps and were dropped over the Mur valley. We flew with a Polish pilot who dropped us from 10,000 feet instead of 1,000, and it took ages before we reached the ground. We found ourselves at Scheifling, a small town more than 40 miles from the spot where we should have landed. And by the time I was down we were no longer a unit. There had been six of us; I'd lost the other five and didn't see them again till after the war. I came down near the Mur River, and nearly drowned in it. Before jumping we were told that there was a river and our rendezvous would be on the far bank. So when I came down in the middle of the night I saw some water and thought this was the little river. I wanted to swim across it, but the water was deeper and deeper, it was up to my chin already. I thought, this can't be the same river, and made my way back. It took me days to get dry again.

The German army was then still in existence. Our mission was to take over the air base of Zeltweg before the Russians could do so. I knew I had to get there, and from my landing point I made my way to that destination. Our task included finding out if the Austrians wanted to make themselves independent, if they were willing to cooperate with us British. On the farms there was hardly a person to be found. There was an old grandfather of 70 and a young granddaughter of about 30, and she had a few children. All the men had gone — every man between 10 and 60. They were all with the Wehrmacht. I didn't find anyone who could do anything at all. The grandfather was old and crippled, and the rest were either babies or mothers. On the other hand, they did not hand me over to the police or the Wehrmacht. I always felt secure. I was always able to buy bread and bacon, and I managed. This went on for some time. I had a sleeping bag, and there were also some alp huts where I stayed, but there I had to be careful. Thus I moved from one farmstead to another, in the direction of Zeltweg. I had a radio with me, but had lost the transmitter and could only receive. I listened to the news and knew how the war was going. The whole business was rather ridiculous — after all, what could a man walking through the forests do on his own? Nothing.

Eventually I got to Zeltweg — on a fire engine I'd requisitioned. It was the only vehicle that still had any gas. I was driven by the mayor of Scheifling. Throughout the journey he was trying to convince me that he'd been against the Nazis. He told me how kind he'd been to the foreign laborers — which made me fear the worst. On our journey we passed through the small town of Judenburg,[1] which struck me as funny in my situation at the time. I then drove right up to that air base and said, I wish to speak to the commanding officer. I was taken to his office and I said that I was a lieutenant in the Eighth Army and wanted this air base to be handed over to me before the Russians got there. He was a cavalry captain — I don't remember his name. He said he didn't dare do this on his own; he'd have to discuss it with the others. So we had a great conference in the evening, with all the senior SS and police chiefs, and all the local bigwigs. It was very interesting to speak to those people; every one of them wanted to speak to me personally. They said, "Herr Lieutenant, may I have a private word with you?" And I said, "Of course, Herr Gauleiter." So we walked over to the window and they all, one bigwig after another, said to me, "I love the Jews. I have a relation, you know, a Jewish relation whom I shielded right through the war. I hope this will be taken into consideration after the war." I said, "Yes, I'm sure it will."

The Germans were very much afraid of the Russians, but the captain was even more afraid of his own people. He said he couldn't hand over command of the airfield to me and sent me to Linz to General Rendulic. He provided me with a car and a major, and we drove to Linz. It was an adventurous drive, and on the way we were attacked by Russian planes. When I got to Linz, Rendulic's ADC told me I could have the airfield. So we drove back, but on the way through the Gesäuse we found ourselves among mutinous Austrian troops.[2] These were troops who'd returned from Russia and Hungary. They'd had enough and didn't want to fight any more. I stayed with these troops for a while and they requested me to drive to the Americans, who'd come up from Munich-Salzburg, and tell them that mutinous Austrian troops needed them. That was shortly before the end of the war, at the beginning of May. I was given a car again, actually it was the same one, and I drove over to the Americans and informed them of the situation. As far as the front line I had a German driver. Then I was sent across a bridge, and on the other side were the Americans. That must have been somewhere near Munich. Naturally, I wasn't able to renew contact with Zeltweg. The war was over for me.

After the end of the war I spent another year at Bad Oeynhausen, which was the headquarters of the British army, and there I was in the War Crimes Investigation Unit. That was quite interesting work, too. I had several cases, such as the Neuengamme case, which was a concentration camp near Hamburg, and the case of the Tesch & Stabenow Company, who'd made Zyklon B gas for the SS.[3] In September 1946 I was finally back in England. I was a major by then, but the next day I was a student again. I continued my chemical engineering studies at the University of Loughborough, a small university in Leicestershire.

I would have quite liked to have gone back to Vienna; after all, I've never been back there. But I'd only go back if I were to be officially invited. If the Austrians said, "Come back. You're welcome here; we'd like to see you again"—in that case I'd go back. But I'm not going back as a private person. I've never received any word from Austria, never anything official from Austria.

In my youth things had been fine. But the Austrians behaved very badly, especially toward my father, who had been a lieutenant in the old imperial army. He'd fought in Russia and in Italy, on the Isonzo [River], on the Piave [River]. One might have assumed that a man who'd fought for his country belonged to it. He had some very splendid decorations, like the Great Silver Medal for Gallantry — I still have that today. My father never received any thanks, although he'd done so much for Austria, and that's very bad. If I were invited now, I'd probably go there with my wife. But I'd also be a little afraid: It can be very painful when 50-year-old memories come flooding back — there I went to school, there I had coffee, there my aunt used to live, or my grandmother, my mother's mother. She was deported to Auschwitz. I'm not sure it would be a good idea.[4]

Annette Saville
England

Annette Saville, born as Annie Bankier on November 21, 1923, in Vienna. Attended primary school and Realgymnasium Novaragasse up to the fifth form and had five years of piano instruction. Escaped to England by children's transport on December 10, 1938. In several homes until August 1939, then underwent eight months' treatment for nervous breakdown. Resumed schooling; completed with O Levels. Worked as hospital and children's nurse, 1943–50, then shorthand typist and secretary, and later as translator with National Westminster Bank. Resumed piano study in her spare time; passed piano teacher exam at the Royal College of Music, 1960. Retired in 1983. Since then fully dedicated to music.

My parents came from Poland. My grandfather died when my mother was two, and my grandmother brought three children under ten to Vienna. My parents were married in 1921, and I was born in 1923. I can remember quite clearly — I was a young girl of perhaps nine or ten then — that my parents took me along to a May Day procession. Suddenly some Nazis appeared and shouted: "Judah, perish! Judah, perish!" My parents quickly led me away. When I was about 12 or 13 my father once took me along to a football match, Baden against Salzburg. The referee was a Viennese and moreover a Jew. Each time the Salzburgers thought he'd made a wrong decision they shouted "Jewish pig! Jewish pig!" at him.

After the Night of Broken Glass we began to sell everything in our house. We realized that we couldn't remain there. The piano and the radio were sold, so there were no more piano lessons. The piano was my great love. My parents were beginning to sell their wardrobes and to get ready for emigration. I left on my own, with a children's transport, from Vienna's Westbahnhof. In Nuremberg a photographer from the Nazi paper *Der Stürmer* came aboard in order to photograph the Jewish-looking children. I had pale eyes and no crooked nose; I didn't look particularly Jewish. But they wanted to take pictures of the children who did look Jewish. Then we moved on until we got to the frontier. At the frontier station a Nazi came aboard and said, "We're only making spot checks. If anyone has anything illegal with them the whole train goes back to Vienna!" So we waited and waited, and eventually the train moved off—back, then forward again and again back. Were we going back to Vienna? At last it continued, and all of us children cheered. And the scout uniforms were brought out, which had been forbidden under Hitler. The Dutch waved to us at the stations, gave us cocoa and bread, and were very good to us. They welcomed us all along our journey through Holland. Some of the children actually remained in Holland.

We next boarded a ship to Harwich. I can remember that in a cabin a small child of five was put in my care. And I recall the steward coming in and me testing my English for the first time: "How many biscuits can we have?" As many as we wanted—I couldn't believe it. We arrived in Harwich in the morning—and what a difference there was in the welcome. Half a dozen gruff Englishmen were standing at the station, staring at us and not saying a word. We then went by train along the coast to Lowestoft, to our first camp. And what did we see there? A big W.H. Smith bookstore, full of copies of Hitler's *Mein Kampf*. We looked at each other: For heaven's sake, where had we come to? Hitler's *Mein Kampf*!

After a few days all the girls were moved to another camp, under the directorship of Anna Essinger. She called the girls together and said, "There is no training for you here, no schooling. All that England can offer you is either domestic work or at best to become a hospital nurse." A poor outlook. But there were also concerts at the camp. There was one woman, Lotte Kalischer, who was a violin teacher. I took part in the concerts, and Lotte Kalischer came along and said, "There is an English family who'd like to take in a musical boy or girl and enable them to get a musical training. Did I want to go there?" But before I could say, "Yes, please," she went on: "Don't go there; you can't make a living from music in England." She'd been in England a few years, and I thought she knew a little more than me. And who do you think went there instead of me? Peter Schidlof, now of the Amadeus Quartet! He received the training which I didn't receive. I never had the same chance again, never. I had to take my piano teacher's exam at age 36. I missed a unique opportunity. And it was all the fault of that woman who advised me against it.

The camp at Dovercourt was horribly cold — everybody remembers that. We were in huts without any heating, we had only an old-fashioned water heater. One night I woke up at two o'clock and found myself standing up to my ankles in water. All the pipes had burst, and we children suffered frostbite. In January 1939 we were gradually moved into children's homes. I was so unhappy in England that I wrote to my parents to ask if I could join them. They had got out shortly after me, and I already had their address in Shanghai. But then came a disappointing letter from my mother. She always was overanxious: "Think it over carefully! Once you are in Shanghai, you will never get back to England." But who wants to be in England where they have treated us so shabbily? I replied: "All right, I'll wait here till September. If I am still in a home then, or in service, I'm coming to Shanghai." And what happened in September? The war started.

About February 1939 I was sent to a family in Suffolk. He was a doctor and she was a doctor too. They had been told, "If the child doesn't suit you, you can send her back!" After three weeks they did send me back. This wrecked my whole life. I have always been afraid I wouldn't be wanted and would be sent back. About August I was moved to another home, where things were much quieter, but I had a nervous breakdown. I spent eight months at the Lady Chichester Hospital for psychiatric patients. There I saw the worst. There was a boy of 13, who'd been in 13 families and two children's homes. He was mentally disturbed and had to be moved to the psychiatric clinic. I think he was disturbed for life. And we had a girl who was half–Jewish; she was 20. She'd also had a nervous breakdown when she was only 16. And there was a nurse who couldn't stand either of us. She said to me, "Whenever I look at your face I see Hitler!" I said, "You're mistaken: I haven't got a drop of German blood in me." Very odd.

After some time in the hospital I managed to get back into secondary school. But the year was full of upheavals. At the hospital there had been children with various infectious diseases, so I was in quarantine for a while. My school friends used to send me work, so I could study on my own. Thus I managed to get back into school. But then I had to have my appendix removed. That was the time of the German campaign in France, and the English became hysterical. I was still in the hospital when everyone called me a spy. They didn't know the difference between a genuine refugee and an enemy — all Germans and Austrians were officially enemies. Then I was sent to a family. But suddenly came orders that within three days all refugees had to be moved from a 20-mile zone of the coast. They were afraid we would help the Germans. So I had to move again. For two weeks I was accommodated with friends in London, and then I came to two Quaker women, two sisters. One ran a small school and the other kept house for her. There I again had a few piano lessons, but suddenly the Blitz began, all that bombing. The two ladies were afraid. They couldn't stand it any longer and moved to Berkshire, west of London. They put me in a Quaker home. Back, therefore, into a home. This was Battle, [near] Speen near Newbury. But somehow they saw to it that I got schooling again, so that I could catch up on my lost year. Actually, I'd lost two years: During the first year in England I wasn't at school at all, and during the second I missed so much.

At age 18 I finally started work. My first job was with Brook Bond, the tea company; that was in 1943. For that I was sent to a new family. I never had a permanent home: I stayed with these people for three months then again I lived somewhere else. Then the woman unexpectedly had another child and needed the room I slept in. I had been with no end of families and in no end of homes. After that I paid for myself.

I don't like saying so, but the English were very mean to us children. For instance, before the war, in Tunbridge Wells. We were poor children without our parents. We only had one schilling a week pocket money. I sent all the money I could spare to my parents in Shanghai to help them. And on the "common," the piece of land that belongs to everyone, where people can go and take what they want, there were raspberries, and we children ate them. But Miss Martha, our warden, came round and said would we please not eat those raspberries; they were for poor English people. People living along the common had forbidden it. They'd written a letter asking her to tell us. While I was at that home Lady Reading visited — the widow of Lord Reading. She was Jewish and not musical. She needed two cheap kitchen maids. I'd been helping in the kitchen, and as I was standing there she walked straight up to me and asked if I wanted to be her kitchen maid. Everyone held their breath because I really was a good pianist. Fortunately Miss Martha said, "She prefers to play the piano," and the lady lost interest in me. She took two others, and they weren't very happy in her service, they wrote to us afterwards.

I therefore didn't have a very pleasant life here. Unfortunately there is anti–Semitism in England, too, not only in Germany and Austria. In 1952 I heard Oswald Mosley speak in Trafalgar Square.[5] Some of his followers were sitting on the lions, keeping watch and shouting, "Judah, perish!" In 1952! British Nazis! I was once in Soho, on a Saturday, and there the English skinheads paraded with their shaven heads, shouting, "Sieg Heil!" I was standing there with a Jewish friend who had a stall in the market, selling poultry, and he said that was the last straw for him. He packed up there and then and went home. English boys shouting "Sieg Heil!"—it seems hardly believable.

Inga Joseph
Sheffield

Inga Joseph, born as Inga Pollak on March 9, 1927, in Vienna. Attended grade school and one year's Gymnasium (at the famous "Schwarzwaldschule"); after the Anschluss, "Jewish school" in Sechskrügelgasse. Escaped to England, June 22, 1939; attended school in Falmouth (Cornwall) until 1944, and spent two years in secretarial college in Oxford. Employed as librarian. Married 1952 (one son); due to husband's job, moved to Sheffield 1963. Trained as teacher of German, 1968–1971. From 1971 until retirement (1991), worked at a comprehensive school and in adult education.

The year 1938 was a decisive one. My father happened to be in Milan and didn't return to Vienna. But otherwise life continued normally for me, and I can't say that I was unhappy — except that I had to change schools and no longer had any parties, and that there were flags everywhere. I knew this was somehow against me, but I didn't quite know in what way. Yet I never experienced any anti–Semitism or anything like it for myself, I only knew about it from others. My father wasn't there and my mother had her hands full running the household and, for a time, also the business. There were friends who were sent to Dachau or suchlike, but somehow this didn't affect me; I simply couldn't believe or understand it. I simply went to school and had my friends. Of course I could no longer go into shops; we would go on a walk and couldn't go to our chocolate shop because there was a notice: "Dogs and Jews not allowed." But I didn't feel personally affected because I wasn't aware that I was Jewish. Or rather, I knew it all right, but the whole business was so strange to me; we'd never been practicing Jews.

Suddenly, therefore, I had this Jewish identity. Suddenly I couldn't go into shops any more, I couldn't ride on the tram, I couldn't go to the cinema — it was like a joke. Nothing ever happened to me, but of course it did to friends. We had a lodger, a Dr. Seifert, who was 40. With my 11 years I was so much in love with him! And one day he didn't return home. He'd been arrested, and it was then that something clicked in me. Two days later he came back: He didn't want to talk about it at all and left immediately. He immigrated to Shanghai. As I've said, we were no Orthodox Jews. My father was totally "anti"; my mother would probably have liked to keep some observances, but she couldn't. It was explained to me that only uneducated Jews were religious. After the Anschluss and expulsion I didn't find any access to the Hebrew religion either; on the contrary, one would have only attracted attention. I don't remember having worn a Star of David; only in my passport there was some nonsense about "Sarah" — I still have that passport. Many of my relatives committed suicide, mainly the elderly ones — my grandfather, my aunt, and others as well. But this was later, when we were already in England. I also lost my grandmother. And of course my mother — that was the worst. But this was 1938, everything was unreal, comical, not really taken seriously. Only when we got to England did I realize that the whole business was not merely comical — but not really until then. The children's transport, for instance, was an adventure for me: My mother would follow, we would go to an English school and learn English — it was an adventure, nothing more. Each day we waited for the postman to bring a coveted document, the affidavit. The experience of departure was like a bad dream — the first time I said goodbye to my mother, the first time I was all alone with strange children. The whole journey was the beginning of a bad dream for me. Some of the children were lucky and were happy with a nice family. But not me, unfortunately, and that's why it was so bad, even though the people did everything for us. I kept a diary into which I poured my whole nostalgia, my whole yearning for Vienna and my mother.

My sister and I were not very close. She was three years older than me and wanted to become an Englishwoman as quickly as possible, but I suffered from nostalgia, huge homesickness. I was very attached to our mother. Mother didn't know that I never wanted to leave Austria, that I would much rather have stayed with her and died with her in a concentration camp. I thought that would be quick and what I was going through was so slow. I have mainly bad memories of that time. Then the family had a baby. As so often happens, they couldn't have children of their own and so they adopted us. But as soon as we got there she became pregnant, and then they didn't want us anymore. We were moved to other people, where we were very happy; that was a lovely time, and it lasted for six months. Then we had to go back. But when the baby was born, we were finally handed over, to those other people. They accepted children from split homes, or whose fathers were in the forces, or whose mothers had too many children. They were two elderly ladies who ran a kind of home, but it was very cheerful. That was in Falmouth, Cornwall. They were a Catholic family; they took us with them to church, and I acted as if I were a Catholic English girl.

The war... I remember the outbreak of the war, Chamberlain's radio address on Sunday, and that we then realized we wouldn't see our parents for a long time. That was the worst of it — that we could no longer write to each other. My father was in Italy first, but had to disappear from there when Mussolini's anti–Semitism began. So he went to France. In 1940, after the fall of France, he got to England by the last ship. By mere chance he got to Plymouth, which is only about 60 miles from Falmouth. So we saw our father again that year. Actually, it was a terrible meeting. He was disappointed with us and we with him. Naturally we believed that he had killed our mother by not getting her out, and this I believe to this day — that it was his fault she was killed there. It hadn't been a very good marriage, and one can't blame politics for everything. But of course this was one reason why he escaped to Italy so readily and without her. In England my father had to join the army, the Pioneer Corps. Needless to say, he had no money. He came with one blanket, which I still have, and the clothes he stood up in. He literally arrived by the last boat. We had to buy him a handkerchief, a hairbrush, and such, with our pocket money. He had a little room somewhere in Falmouth. Try to picture it: A man who had always been independent, with his own apartment and library, now had to rely on his children, like a beggar, on the children he'd never had a very good relationship with. So it was just as bad for him as it was for us. Besides, I wanted to be completely English and didn't want other people to know that I had such a foreign father, a foreigner and a Jew. I didn't want that. It was a very complex situation.

During those years I had to adapt to English culture and stand on my own feet. I don't want to present this as some special achievement; there was no alternative. I wanted to be just as the others, to be English was something divine. And that's why I feel so guilty — for denying my religion and my mother. None of this existed for me. At the end of the war, when I was in Oxford, there was an Austrian Society there. They had lists. There was a Viennese family in Oxford, a boy and a girl with their parents. I met the boy on his bicycle and he asked me where I was going. I said, "I'm off to the Austrian Society, I want to see the list of people who have disappeared." A few weeks later he asked me what the concert had been like. He thought I'd gone to a Liszt recital. I didn't correct him, but used some excuse. The fact is I didn't want people to know that I had a mother who had disappeared. Actually, I did see that list, but my mother's name was not on it. But I was so ashamed of my background. When my father wanted to marry again at some later date, he had to put an advertisement in the paper. This is when he found out that she was no longer alive. Herr Gattinger, the concierge, reported only that the people were rounded up one day. Many years later there was another advertisement here in Sheffield, and by then my sense of guilt was even greater, but of course it was too late for that. That time they discovered that she had possibly been taken to Russia. But I don't believe it, and what difference does it make?

When the war was over in 1945, this also raised a problem for me. When you've turned into a different person over the past six years and you've tried to forget everything that went before, then the end of the war was something very dramatic because suddenly there was the possibility of returning to your origins. But for me this wasn't possible, I believed that in the meantime I had become an English girl. All that had happened before wasn't really true. How was I to handle that, and what about my mother, for whom, of course, I longed a great deal? And Austria, too— after all, I had been happy there; I'd had a particularly happy childhood. But there was no other way; the bridge had gone. No one encouraged me to do so, and it never occurred to me to go back to Austria. My father felt just the same as the two of us. We were not to tell anyone that we were Jewish. We had to get ourselves baptized. It was a secret, a shameful secret. During the war there had been justified fear of an invasion, and, as we were living near the coast, we were in danger. It was silly to think that this game of hide-and-seek would have any effect, but my father then influenced me a great deal. Certainly we were not to mention our origins. The bridge had quite simply gone and there was no going back for us. But over here we weren't fully accepted either. At school we were strangers from the start, the girls from abroad. This went on for quite a time. In 1945 I was 17 and independent in the sense that I had a job. At my place of work, some of my colleagues knew that I was from Austria. "When did you leave Austria?"

was a constant question. And I found some explanation, probably lies. This was terrible, I probably made things much more difficult for myself than other people in the same position. I lived all that time in a very abnormal situation — I didn't belong here; I had a Jewish identity I didn't wish to reveal because it was dangerous and because I hadn't accepted it myself. And I had no idea how to normalize the situation. All I wanted was to be English.

I no longer used my native language. Later I had to study it from the beginning. Of course, I hadn't entirely forgotten German: At 12, one is too old to forget one's mother tongue. But when we were in Vienna again for the first time, in 1961, I didn't want to know anything about it. I was traveling with my husband and son, who was then five and didn't know anything about it. Everything felt so odd; I was Jekyll and Hyde. We went to our apartment, but of course they didn't let us in. They knew of nothing, and I didn't want to make waves. I believe a veterinary surgeon now lives there. I didn't speak to him, he only just opened the door and wouldn't allow us in. Maybe they were also afraid of burglars.

To this day I don't understand how one can persecute a certain group of people in this manner. Why did everyone have to leave the country? Some were bad, some were good — so why everyone? Why not just the bad ones? was what I probably thought. Austria was the first scene of my happiness. The country, holidays, Christmas, birthday parties, my girlfriends, everything except that bad marriage. And the spring! The feeling of spring in Vienna has never left me — the air, the scent of lilac in the Arenberg Park. Other people, my sister for instance, have quite different stories to tell. But these were my earliest memories, and this suited me. I have never tried to tell my son anything about this. He never knew anything, and now I have inhibitions. At one time, when he was about ten, I tried to tell him who I really was by writing stories in a copybook. Or more correctly, I dictated them and it was he who wrote, because he had terrible handwriting and was supposed to practice. We still have the copybook. I felt guilty and thought my son should know who I was. My husband, too, didn't know for a long time that I was Jewish. I couldn't tell him. He's a Catholic, but not religious. So I wrote a story for the boy — about a man called "Madolf Shitler" who persecuted all people with dark hair. And somehow in this story I reported what had happened. I don't think it made sense to him. Nor has he ever asked any questions; he probably sensed that it was a secret, something we don't talk about. But he's got to know. I'm sure it's awful of me.

I'd love to know who it was went to our apartment on Wipplinger-strasse and picked up my mother. I would have liked to speak to that person, to ask him, "How could you do such a thing? She was such a nice, kind, innocent lady!" This would have helped me. I have asked around who that man was and how I could find him. But nobody knew, and of course he's probably dead now. That's what I'm thinking. Silly, trivial things.

Does Austria mean anything to me? Yes, I think so. It's awful, I would so much like to be accepted in Austria, to hear from someone: "Ah, here you are again. I'm so sorry." I'd like that, but nobody says so. They close the door on you. They are not unfriendly. I never experienced any anti–Semitism, never. I'd like to hear some older person say, "It would be nice if you came back." That would be my greatest happiness — if someone there cared about me. That was the land where I was born. If only they said, "Yes, this is your country, too!" Because over here people still ask me, to this day, "When are you going home, to Austria?"

Caroline Warren
London

Caroline Warren, born July 31, 1904, in Znojmo (Znaim),
Moravia. Attended local grade and secondary schools, followed
by commercial college. Following the early death of her parents,
she moved to Vienna in 1922. Married, 1925 (Weintraub). Lived
in Vienna's 2nd District. Her husband narrowly avoided arrest in
April 1938 by escaping to Prague, but was later deported by the
Nazis to a concentration camp and murdered. She entrusted her
10-year-old son to an English children's transport in July 1939 and
soon after followed him. Worked as domestic worker in Pangbourne, later in Gloucester, while her son was in a Quaker home.
From June 1940 to May 1941, interned (Holloway Prison and Isle
of Man). Following release from internment, she worked as a waitress and in the armaments industry. Granted British citizenship,
1949. From 1949 until retirement in 1967, employed in the export
division of a big London department store. Repeatedly traveled
to Austria to establish what happened to her husband, received
certain confirmation of his death in 1958. Thereupon changed her
name from Karola Weintraub to Caroline Warren. Died in 1995.

My name was originally Weintraub, until 1945. Austria always claimed
it had been overrun; this wasn't true. I saw with my own eyes how Hitler
was welcomed, how he was cheered when he moved in. One had to hang
out flags, even Jewish people had to hang out swastika flags because the
Germans moved down Praterstrasse. I was there and saw them. The people were jubilant. And when Hess was there: "Dear Rudi, be so kind / and
show yourself at the window!" The women were like crazy. But the whole
nation was like that. I lived on Praterstrasse, opposite the synagogue. And
what do you think the women yelled when they saw it burning? "Throw
in all the Jews! Into the burning synagogue!"

My husband was the greatest good fortune in my life. He was an Austrian and felt like an Austrian. "This one's a Jew and that one's a Christian" just didn't exist then, at least not in our circles. And soon after the Anschluss, he had to escape. We happened to be in the Café Häger on Praterstrasse at the time, and the proprietor came round and said, "Herr Weintraub, you'd better disappear. The Gestapo were here, looking for you. They don't know where you live. They only said the blonde woman with the baby carriage and the dog." That same night he was off, with nothing but his briefcase, across the Czech frontier. All the tenants in the building were Jews, all very friendly; many of them escaped like my husband — with nothing but a briefcase. You paid a man to guide you through the forest. The next day my husband phoned me to say he got across the frontier all right. And who came to see me? The Gestapo. Where was my husband? I said he isn't here. This was repeated several more times.

Some time later they wanted to arrest my neighbors. I knew my neighbors were just visiting their grandparents to say goodbye to them. I managed to warn them that their flat was just being searched. I thought that as a non–Jew I could do that. When I got back home my landlady was waiting for me: "Frau Weintraub, what on earth have you done? The Gestapo's looking for you!" Now that was terrible. They'd taken the child, Kurt, with them, he was to tell them where his mother was. But he didn't know. I was in a panic. I had to collect the child from the Gestapo. There they said, "Ah yes, we've seen this before. The Jews have always snapped up the pretty women, the blondes." And of course they reviled me. But they handed the child over because I pretended that I didn't know anything. That same night my neighbors got away illegally, crossing the frontier into Hungary.

Eventually I also managed to get out. I had to be secretive about it because they were after me. A recently moved-in neighbor had already denounced me once before, no doubt the same who one night chalked WHORE on our front door. He used to be a Communist and now he was a Fascist, and I'd accused him of that. I went to the English Quakers — they were in Wollzeile. Everything there was topsy-turvy. The fact was that I had absolutely nothing — no emigration papers, no invitation, no permit, nothing of what one needed to get out. So I registered my boy for a children's transport, to get him out first. Simultaneously I offered myself as a courier for a transport, but not for the same one. No one was to know that we belonged together. I had to keep everything secret.

In July 1939, my son got to England with the Quakers, and a week

later I traveled myself with children and babies. That was a frightful journey. A Gestapo man came aboard and locked the carriage door, looked at
me and asked what I was doing there. I said I intended to visit someone
in England and then return. Of course they reviled me. But because I was
accompanying two babies, I managed to get to England.

I found a job as a domestic in a place called Pangbourne, with a titled
lady. For my interview I was fairly well dressed; she probably thought I
couldn't work. But I was a very good worker and she liked that. The house
stood on its own like a chateau. I didn't know where to go, where to get
advice. I knew no English, and I was among nothing but English people
without even knowing the language. And I wanted to see my son, to help
him. The boy was up in the North, in a Quaker orphanage. And I had gone
to England chiefly so that we could be together.

Then the war broke out. Naturally, without a permit I could not make
any more visits. Before the war we had not been regarded as enemies. On
the radio they always said, "Don't trust people from Austria, Germany, or
wherever; they could be enemy aliens and not real refugees from persecution." That, of course, was very bitter, because at first I had been quite
popular as an Austrian. When I got here I wrote to my husband that I was
very unhappy. And he wrote back that I should return to Vienna: "They're
not going to last long, the Nazis. You go back and I'll join you there!" He
was so trusting, he still hadn't realized the true situation in Austria. I didn't
stay long with that titled lady because I wanted to be nearer to my child,
and so I went to an old lady in Gloucester. I had a feeling that from there
I could more easily look after the child and be in touch with the outside
world. At the titled lady's I was surrounded by high walls.

The internments began in 1940. First one went to court and was
classified as a "friendly alien" or "enemy alien." But I had learned English
very quickly and had mixed with people, and someone — this is what the
judge told me — had denounced me. Probably just because of my blond
hair. I always did look like a typical German. First I spent four months in
Holloway Prison, together with ordinary women criminals, and subsequently eight months on the Isle of Man. It was terrible. I wrote one letter after another to get out. But it took ages before anything started
moving. I was eventually freed after a hearing by a tribunal. The judge,
to whom I told everything, shook my hand and wished me better luck in
the future. Of course I had no money when I was released, so I first went
back to the old lady until I had saved up a little. Then I went to the orphanage where my son was, because the Quaker school had meanwhile been

disbanded. Most of the teachers had gone to Canada — incidentally, the ship by which they traveled went down. I saw quite a number of children and thought that my child could not possibly be among them. Because they were all in a frightful state. The boy was in a totally neglected condition — I ordered a taxi and virtually abducted him. Then I went to London with him because my employer wanted a servant without dependents. In London I worked as a waitress at a Lyons Corner House, where most of the staff were foreigners like me. We had to work hard and lived mainly from our tips. I kept my child with me. One day when I got home I was told the police had been round because I had abducted the child from the orphanage. I told them how horrified I'd been at the way he looked, that's why I'd taken him away. I was summoned for a hearing and had to repeat all that, and I said if I had known what would happen to my child and to me I'd never have come to England.

I didn't know what school to send my boy to; after all, I had no money. I had to work and I earned very little. The officials wanted to find him a place as an apprentice because he was already 15, but I was horrified and got terribly worked up. If I'd known that, I wouldn't have come to England. That prison! And internment! The way the child looked! My statements evidently impressed the senior official. He was a very nice person and asked me what I wanted. I answered, "For myself nothing at all, I am capable of working, but I want a future for my son. He's only got me, he's got to have a future!" I didn't yet know then what had happened to my husband. So this man offered him the opportunity of entering a technical college, provided he passed an exam. But that wasn't so simple. After his stay at the orphanage my son was disturbed, almost confused, certainly totally changed. One might have thought that he wasn't my child at all. I had to talk to him a great deal; I had to study with him so he might pass his exam. This we did all in my free time. And eventually he passed and got into that college. I was very happy; it was the first positive thing that had happened to me in England.

While I still had a hope of finding my husband, I went to Austria every year, as soon as I had saved some money, to search for him. When the money gave out I returned to England. In 1958 I received the news of his death from the Red Cross, and I had a nervous breakdown. That's when I changed my name from Weintraub to Warren and resolved to stay in England. In Austria no one had helped me — I was even shouted at. When I wanted to retire I went to the Austrian consulate again to ask whom to turn to in order to get an apartment in Austria. The man yelled at me, "I

wouldn't mind an apartment in Austria and another in England," whereupon I burst into tears and left. The man ran after me, he was probably
sorry, and asked if I didn't want help. "I need no help from you!" But one
of the consuls, a lawyer, was most charming to me; he wanted to help me
settle in Austria again. But nothing came of it.

I still have nightmares. I must climb over mountains and there are
ravines, and I don't know if I should cross them. Sometimes I am at a railway station, about to travel somewhere, and suddenly I am in a strange
country, I don't know anybody, I don't know the street, I am lost, and I
am afraid I won't find my way back home. When I wake up I am thankful to be in my bed.

Dorothy Fleming
Sheffield

Dorothy Fleming, born May 3, 1928, as Dorli Oppenheimer in Vienna. Completed the mandatory school and began attending the Frauenerwerbsverein school up to her escape to England on January 19, 1939. Continued schooling in Leeds, Whitchurch (Wales), Westbury (Wiltshire) and Llandaff (Wales). Trained as a teacher in Bath, 1946–48; worked in London (1948–50), Brighton (1951), Mexborough (1951–59) and Sheffield. Married in 1949 and had three children. In 1973, following study of psychology (1968–71) and further research, became a professor at the Sheffield Teachers Training College. Retired on health grounds in 1988.

═══════════════

The Anschluss had immediate consequences for our domestic life. Meals had always been joyful events; we used to tell jokes and stories from the opera, from concerts and from gymnastic classes — and suddenly there were no more jokes, and all the talk was of visas and permits, of who'd managed to get out and — more often that one would think — who'd killed themselves. All fun had gone from our home — I no longer saw my parents smile; their features were always serious. For a while they tried not to speak about it before us children, but that couldn't be kept up because matters had to be discussed. I don't know precisely when, but in November, after the Kristallnacht, they simply took away the shops my father owned. How did this happen? Entirely without warning. A Nazi entered the shop and announced that he now owned the business. Resistance was impossible.

After that my parents made every effort to get out. An optician from Newcastle stood surety for my father and my mother. We don't know exactly when and how. After the Kristallnacht my parents discovered that unaccompanied children could get away. I am not quite clear about the details of this. From documents I have, I know that a family in Leeds wrote to London on November 20 that they were prepared to accept children, and on the very next day the organizations in London passed this on. So I left by train on January 10. There are many entries in my album from the end of December. Mother took us around to say goodbye to relatives and friends — those who had not left yet. On January 12, I arrived in England. Parting can't have been all that bad for me because I'd been away from home a few times before, for skiing and for summer vacations. And besides, my mother told me, "You two go first and we'll follow." Recently, a mere couple of weeks ago, we told her how brave she'd been to send us off on our own, and she said, "It didn't take much courage; I simply knew that we'd follow you." And my husband said, "How could you have been so sure? After all, others lost their lives." Either she believed it so firmly that no other possibility occurred to her, or else this is how she recalls it now — she's 88. When I told her in June 1989 that 95 percent of parents did not follow their children, this made no impression on her at all: "I told you we would come, and we came." My father's mother was sick, and that was probably why she didn't get out so quickly; they wanted to make arrangements for her first. I believe that she moved in with somebody and died in Vienna. We always tried to clear this up, but so far without success.

My maternal grandfather died in Vienna of some illness. But my maternal grandmother was deported and murdered — that is horrible. She was an energetic person, quite wonderful, fantastic, and I think I'm the one who has most taken after her. She was apparently very Jewish and for many years was secretary of a Jewish women's charitable movement in Vienna. I only learned about her fate many years later. But we still have the correspondence between her and her sister in Shanghai.

The journey by "children's transport" was not very alarming for me; I saw it more as an adventure. But I did feel a sense of responsibility for my little sister. I'd been told, "You'll be looking after Lisi. You'll be traveling together with other children and there won't be any grown-ups with you. And in England they won't separate you." And that's how it was. We got to the Westbahnhof late in the evening, and there were a lot of people with children there already. Our parents said, "So long," and "Bye now." We kissed goodbye, and then we lifted my sister up into the luggage net because she was the smallest. The moment she was up there, she was sick, and so I spent the next half-hour cleaning up myself and the compartment, which may have been a good thing because I scarcely noticed the train pulling out. The very small children were up on the luggage racks; the rest were on the seats, and a few even under the seats because the train was so packed. We each had only one piece of luggage. At the frontier we all felt rather uneasy because word had got round that the Nazis would come on board to inspect us. "Be careful" was the slogan. I had no gold or jewelry with me, but in our compartment was a boy of perhaps 10 or 11 whose father had given him a gold pocket watch which had belonged to his grandfather and great-grandfather and which, he'd been told, he could sell in the event of extreme difficulties, though it would be better if he could keep it safe for his descendants. But just before the frontier he panicked, thinking they might discover the watch on him, take it away, and punish him, and so he slipped it into a slot of the ventilator. No one found it, but he couldn't get it out again. All through the journey he tried. We said to him, "Look, your father won't mind. You're safe and that's more important!" We, who were 8, 10 or 12, spoke like old people. "Don't worry about it; it's only a watch!" But he was in a terrible state about his loss.

Then we crossed the frontier, and this is what all "children's transport" children remember: the kind ladies in Holland who welcomed us at the station with orange juice and hot chocolate — just as if we were their own children. In London we were met. We spent the night at the house of an aunt who took us to the train for Leeds the next day. In Leeds we stayed with a young married couple, where I was very happy. There was a lot of laughter and singing. There was a dog and a garden and young happy people. And I could speak English, so it wasn't much of a problem for me. But my sister knew no English at all. She was only four; she'd been told what would happen, but I'm sure she didn't understand. She clung to me the whole time. Our new guest parents thought it would be best for me to go to school and for her to go to a kindergarten so she'd be with other children. I don't know if this was the best. For me it was wonderful. I was at school all day — free from any burden. But my sister was unable to make herself understood; she cried a lot and began to wet her bed again. Things were awful for a while.

My parents got to England toward the end of April and visited us in Leeds. When it became clear that there was no permanent job for my father, and when, after a few weeks, they left Newcastle again, my sister very soon joined them in London. But I stayed on in Leeds with my guest parents a little longer. If my sister had remained with us another two or three months, she would have adjusted to our new environment. But just then our parents arrived and Lisi naturally was angry with them because, as she saw it, they had sent her away. I believe it wrecked her whole life. She was never the same again and in her further life never really got on with people. She made an impossible marriage. Then there was a divorce, and her son has tried twice or three times to kill himself. Sadly she died three years ago, much too soon, at age 52. You might say she died of the long-term effects of a broken heart. The son has pulled himself together, but he is a loner without any friends, and he leads an odd life. And I am sure all this is due to that trauma of separation. My sister was four at the time, which is probably the worst time to be separated from one's parents — I'm speaking now as a mother, not as a psychologist. It seems to me that other children who got here at that tender age likewise suffered a lot, both as children and later as adults.

We were in Austria on a holiday three or four years ago, near Innsbruck, to meet with a friend there and to spend some time near Seefeld. In Innsbruck we made some inquiries, met people, and saw the Jewish assembly room. This was all very interesting and also very moving, because Innsbruck was a nest of Nazis. And now we learned from a Catholic lady in Innsbruck that there is a Provincial Society of the Christian-Jewish Coordination Committee in Innsbruck. Well, this impressed us. But when we had got back to Innsbruck by train from Seefeld, there were a lot of foreigners there. After all it was vacation time; there were a few Israelis and some English people. And along came a local man who said very loudly, "So many foreigners! One should send a few more of them into the gas!" This so annoyed us that we said, "Never again to Austria! There's the whole wide world: Why should we go back to Austria? Never again." My husband was very upset about it. He talked about it to our tour guide, and she was very shocked. She said she'd heard from her brother, who lived in Seefeld, that there are some such people. This was the only time we heard remarks like that, but once is quite enough.

Lilly Sykes
London

Lilly Sykes, born as Lilly Lechner on June 1, 1921, in Berlin to Austrian parents. The family fled from Hitler to Pressburg (Bratislava) in 1934. Attended German-language Realgymnasium; banned from school attendance after the German invasion of Czechoslovakia. In August 1939, escaped with her mother and grandmother to England via Hungary, Yugoslavia, Italy and France. Worked in a factory during the war. After the war, married Robert Ehrenstein (divorced in 1952); married a second time in 1955 to writer John Sykes (died 1987); from that marriage, two sons (born 1957 and 1960). Worked as Montessori kindergarten teacher, 1955 until retirement in 1980. Beginning in 1975, served as honorary courier for the Anglo-Austrian Society's children's vacation exchange program.

We had a German theater in Bratislava in 1938,[6] and I remember how my mother, elegantly dressed, would take the famous tram to Vienna to go to the opera there — that was quite normal. As for political things, such as marches, I didn't take much notice of them — not until after the Anschluss. That I can report on very accurately, because it was the day of my first and last ball. In the middle of the night someone came running in: "The Germans have marched into Austria! We must immediately help our people. Our people are swimming across the Váh!" The Váh River then formed the frontier. We were all members of a swimming club. We ran down there at once and pulled the people out of the water, those who weren't such good swimmers. If I remember rightly, they were about twenty people. This was in the night after the Anschluss. They were fired on — I don't know whether by Austrians or whether the Germans had got there already. A friend of mine, the son of a famous cartoonist, who had already run away from Vienna together with his family, got a bullet in the leg. There was no sign of any Czechoslovak gendarmes. We didn't try to alert anybody: we were frightened ourselves when the firing started. We took the people home with us; none of them wanted the police to know. In Bratislava everything changed overnight. The next day all the Christian children were wearing cornflowers — so it was instantly obvious who was a Christian and who was a Jew. This was the first time. In the break, I ran outside with a friend to buy cornflowers and we pinned those on ourselves and that was the end of it.

Suddenly the whole situation was politicized. One person was suddenly a German Nazi, another was a Slovak, yet another a Hungarian. The atmosphere was frightful. The teachers were shaking with fear. Discrimination of the Jews then started at a stroke. Everything was turned upside down after that night; suddenly there were two camps, friends and enemies. All the Jewish children were expelled from the German Realgymnasium, except those in their final year. Fred Mauner, who lived close to us, was still allowed to graduate. We were all chucked out; I was then in the fourth form. Some of the students changed over to Slovak schools. My grandmother was acquainted with an Englishwoman who invited her to London. Of course it was very complicated to get a visa; there was no British consulate in Bratislava, and she had to travel to Prague. But soon the Germans moved into Prague, too. Everything went so fast. My mother was saying we couldn't remain there, we had to go. I left school therefore and went somewhere to learn a little needlework and cooking. A lot of people tried to go to Palestine illegally by ship. I would have quite liked to go there myself, but my mother was no Zionist, and also there were three of us — my mother, my grandmother and myself. My father had long gone off to Brazil with another woman. My grandmother was lucky enough to get to London as the courier of a children's transport.

It then took her until August 1939 to get us to England. We only got out at the last moment: We were in Bratislava until August 10, 1939. With our passports, we needed a visa — and we didn't get it. "Come again if you like, but..." was what we invariably heard. We knew about everything that had been happening across the frontier in Vienna; we had a great many relatives there. People were escaping any way they could — over the frontier, over the mountains, by ship illegally down the Danube, in every conceivable manner, everybody for himself. This was what happened after the Anschluss. I cannot recall that there had been any fear before then. After all, Germany was a long way off.

I got to England on August 18, 1939. I was 16 then. I never went back to school; that was my misfortune. In England compulsory education finished at 14, and I was beyond that age, so no one was concerned about me any longer. Those below 14 were placed in schools, like my friend Erich. If you were over 14, no one bothered about you. We didn't know English, and we didn't know our way about. Luckily there were those big refugee organizations like Bloomsbury House, because we were totally helpless. Every refugee could register there, and every week we received a little money, but that was all. And the people were sorted into "friendly aliens" and "enemy aliens." A cousin of mine, who had come from Germany, was therefore immediately interned. They simply interned everybody. My mother and I were not interned; we were classified as "friendly aliens" because we had come from Czechoslovakia — the criterion was where a person came from. As late as the end of August, people were still being sent back from Dover because they had no visas and no one to sponsor them. I said recently, "But the British did accept 10,000 children." And Erich said, "Sure, they each had a guarantee of 50 pounds, else they wouldn't have been allowed in!" We were also sponsored, not by grandmother, but by her friend. Without sponsorship no one got in. The British sent people back from Dover — to their certain deaths! And that's a fact; let no one claim that this isn't true. Not everything was as great as one might imagine.

My husband was the first Englishman I met, and that was in 1954. I never had anything to do with English people. The Austrians and Czechs were living quite apart from the English, and there was no real contact. Girls like me had never learned anything. Oh yes, we were good at Latin! There were some people who had come over earlier, and they already owned small factories. They employed us for sewing on buttons and such like. It was frightful — you can't imagine. But then we didn't know anything and were no use for anything. And we didn't know any English. During the war, therefore, we did what work there was, mostly sewing, making uniforms, ironing, sewing on buttons, that kind of thing. There was the Pioneer Corps, of course, but not for women. There was no one who said, "Come, we've got work for you!" No one wanted to know about us; after all, we were foreigners. We had to offer ourselves for work. No English person wanted to employ us. There's a belief that in a war everything is planned, but we didn't notice any of it.

When I was 21, I was called up for the Czech brigade. I was employed with the convoys, the ships which brought all the foodstuffs from America.

Everything had to be calculated—loading, for instance—that was my job. My place of work was in London, in a huge building. There were a hundred women sitting there and all were calculating: "This weighs so-and-so much and needs so-and-so much space…" The Island Force was the name of the firm, a shipping company. That's where I was sent because my French was good. God, it was a muddle, but somehow we all survived it. And I believe that the people who made good in England are really the ones who always used their elbows. We couldn't sink any lower; we could only rise up, as a friend once remarked to me. But this was not the case with everyone; a lot never managed. Take my grandmother, my mother, and myself. My grandmother was 60—what could she do? Nothing any longer. And she was half blind. All the last years, until she died in 1953, she lived on support, made hospital visits and looked after patients. My mother was born in 1900. Of course she never learned anything; in those days women just stayed at home. She was in charge of a refugee club. These people, of course, were all voluntary workers. No one drew any pay; everybody just lived on their support payments. They took a house in Hampstead then—13 men they were, and the women all did the cooking. One could play cards there, and there was an open fire where people could warm themselves. And after the war she was in charge of a large house, also for foreigners. We lived quite isolated lives, which wasn't the case in America, was it?

In 1954 I met my husband, an Englishman, and married him. My parents-in-law treated me like a prostitute. A poor Jewish foreigner? What kind of match was that! That's how it is in England. No point in denying it. I have English friends who refer to me as "my Austrian friend" or "my German friend," and I've been living here for over fifty years. I am not bitter about it, not really. And I always introduce myself as "I'm a bloody foreigner" to take the wind out of their sails. But I do regret that we didn't go straight to America at the time; that was a great mistake, also for my generation. I would have continued my schooling, I would have learned something and I would have become an American. Here I can never become English. In England or France it is impossible to integrate.

To return after 1945—no, that was never an option. Our relatives who didn't manage to get out all lost their lives. That's a heavy burden. My mother's cousin went back in 1948—but he very soon returned to England again. He said one couldn't live with ghosts. When everybody you knew perished and you return to where you came from and are all alone, there's no point in staying there. One can't live in the past. Fred

Mauner, who was at school with me, returned in order to search for his people. We all searched. My mother searched through the Red Cross.

Because I am an Anglo-Austrian Society courier for children's exchange transports, I get to Austria two or three times a year, and I enjoy going there. I now have many friends there and feel comfortable there. My children don't know German, which makes a great difference. I can go to a German theater, I can read a German book — I don't want to lose the language. I can't understand people saying, "I don't want to hear a German word ever again." That's not my attitude. I find that somehow this is a part of me. I had wanted, at the time, to teach my children German, but since my husband doesn't know the language, he didn't let me because he wouldn't understand what we were talking about. And that was the end of the matter.

My mother died in 1956 and for the next 20 years I never spoke or heard a German word; the first one eventually came from my aunt. It always depends on how you live, in what circles, whom you meet — everything is chance. My two sons, now grown up, have no interest whatever in discovering anything, they are not interested in ancestors or religion, or in politics — in nothing. But that is today's English generation: They are so disillusioned they don't want to know anything; they only want to make their music or write their books. People like me have lived with the past for 50 years, we have reconciled ourselves to it — or perhaps not, depending on the individual.

The Austrians are now giving an additional pension to everyone who was ten years old on March 11, 1938 — I find that very good. I think that's excellent, because there are many who have absolutely nothing. They are in such tight circumstances that one never sees them. In England many of them only receive a pension of £60 a week, just enough not to starve or to freeze to death. I am hoping that the Austrian state will further reduce the age limit a little,[7] because many children who came over by children's transports were even younger. I made the acquaintance of a Mrs. Erika Kohlmann, who came to England at the age of five and of course never saw her parents again. After the war she went to the authorities in Vienna to find out what happened to her parents, and they showed her some documents: Her mother was deported on such and such a date and gassed on such and such a date. She burst into tears, but they didn't even say, "We're sorry"— that's not right. Personally I would welcome it if they were all compensated. After all, there are so few left, most of them have died. From what I hear, the people who made it to America are far better off, I mean the older people. But in England the people are not treated well. A few have done well and have a fine house and enough money. But there are a great many one doesn't see who are very badly off. Something should be done for these people. Of course, one can't make full reparations; one can't turn back history.

The Waldheim business has affected me in the sense that a great many acquaintances, especially English ones, not Jews, have come to me and said, "Well, now you can't ever travel to Austria again!" I say, "Why not, what do I care about Waldheim?" And they don't understand and look at me oddly. How could I do this, surely this was a scandal; I should now travel to Greece or Italy. But so long as the Anglo-Austrian Society needs me to accompany the exchange-program children, I'll do it. Waldheim can take a running jump! But the whole business did a great deal of harm to the Anglo-Austrian Society. We used to have two flights a week, but since the Waldheim affair there's been only one a week. A great many English people said they weren't sending their children to a country where such a man is president. It did a lot of harm to Austria.

I experienced strong anti–Semitism here, in England, for the first time when I married my English husband. The reaction of my parents-in-law was very bad. Another example: My elder son was very good at school and I wanted him to go to a particular public school. We went there to present ourselves, and I never conceal my identity. I said straightaway who I was and where I came from; I speak perfect English, so I wouldn't have to, but I do it on principle. And we were told: "We are very sorry, but our admission quota for Jewish children is limited to 20 percent." My son then went to a Quaker school. And from my English acquaintances I also, time and again, hear such remarks. Once I walked in the park with a woman friend from the next street, and we both remarked how beautiful it was to be living in Richmond. I said there were really only two beautiful neighborhoods in London, Hampstead and Richmond. Whereupon she said, "My dear, you mustn't live in Hampstead, it's full of Jews!" And I said: "I am sorry, dear friend, but you are walking with a Jewess; would you like me to cross to the other side of the street?" I never saw her again. In other words, to experience anti–Semitism I don't have to travel to Austria. I can get that right here.

Sir Ernst Gombrich

As there were no prospects of employment for me in Vienna, I accepted the research engagement of the Warburg Institute and came to London at the beginning of 1936. Even then I was hoping that I might be able to stay here. In the autumn of 1936, I got married. I was granted leave by the Institute so that I could finish the book I was writing jointly with Ernst Kris, and on that occasion we married. My wife comes from Bohemia. When the book was finished, we both returned to London in February 1937. Our son was born here in England. Then came the notorious meeting between Schuschnigg and Hitler on the Obersalzberg,[8] and Seyss-Inquart[9] became minister of the interior. We were terribly worked up and telephoned my parents in Vienna. They didn't understand anything at all and, on the contrary, thought it was time for us to come back to Vienna again. There was nothing we could do: They simply didn't understand the magnitude of the danger now that Seyss-Inquart was minister of the interior. In the end, my parents managed to get out, but nearly all the relatives of my wife lost their lives, and so did my mother's brother. My father never then thought of emigrating: He had his work, and leaving the country never occurred to him at all.

Now there was a comical instance of good luck, if one can call it that. My mother had a piano pupil who was very fond of her, a Bulgarian lady, to whom she gave a letter of recommendation when that lady was about to leave Vienna. As she was crossing the frontier illegally, she was arrested and the frontier guards found my mother's letter. Mother was summoned to the Gestapo to explain her letter. The Gestapo were very polite with her and said, "But, dear lady, you ought to be careful; it's people like you we need," and so on. But it came as a shock to her nevertheless. My father had been a Freemason. That too was a dangerous thing, and for some time they confiscated his passport because of it. These two incidents then convinced my parents that, totally against their expectation, life for them couldn't continue in Austria. So we tried over here to get a guarantee for my parents. It wasn't easy, and it also wasn't pleasant, as you can imagine. My mother even got a work permit to give piano lessons over here, and this was due to the wife of Arturo Toscanini, who used her influence for her. We had known the Toscaninis, and he'd visited us once. Toscanini's wife invited me to see her, and it was all enormously touching. My mother, in consequence, was permitted to give piano lessons on condition that she didn't charge less than two guineas for a lesson. That was a great deal of money. She'd had pupils from England even while still living in Vienna, and they wanted to continue studying with her.

Many people are unaware of this, but musicians had the greatest problems of all. There were three professions in England where the professional organizations did not behave too well and opposed refugees: doctors, photographers, and musicians. They were all afraid of competition. There were even some prominent Jewish musicians in England who took up a stance against the refugees with the argument that there were enough unemployed musicians in England — which was perfectly true. I remember a very nice man, a minor piano teacher, saying to me, "To be honest, these people are a threat to me. I admit that they are all better qualified — but what am I to do?" It was the same with the photographers. And medical men, as is well known, had to pass "nostrification" exams. There were famous figures among them. One of the most absurd cases was the famous ear specialist Dr. Neumann, who had treated the Duke of Windsor in Austria but was not allowed to practice in England.

During the war I worked for six years in the Monitoring Service of the BBC, listening in to enemy broadcasts, and it was very hard work and mostly at night. We naturally imagined that we were doing a lot for the war effort. The war was probably won by different means, but now and again it may have made some difference that we were able to hear the German transmitters. We didn't do any broadcasting, we only listened, and every day the Monitoring Service published a fat document in two volumes. For 18 months, I was a monitor myself, later a so-called supervisor, and I played a certain part within the organization. I listened to all of Hitler's speeches and I read all Goebbels's articles in *Das Reich*, and often translated them. There is an amusing story: There was one Hans Fritsche, you might say he was the propaganda clown. He even faced the Allied Tribunal in Nuremberg, instead of Goebbels, who had taken his own life, but he was acquitted because he was a subordinate. Three times a week Hans

Fritsche made a propaganda broadcast; these were all full of little jokes, and we translated them all. And after the war I mentioned to a former schoolmate that I'd heard every one of Fritsche's broadcasts, and he said with surprise, "Funny, I never heard him." That's why I think that we overestimated our role. But of course it had to be, one had to listen to all those things; it was all taken very seriously. I remember the day when Dittmar, the spokesman of the Wehrmacht High Command, admitted that the war was lost. I remember it because no one understood it. He said, "No nation can be expected to take such burdens upon itself — without an aim. We have such an aim — to break the enemy's will to annihilate us." He no longer said "victory." That, I think, was in 1943, after Stalingrad [Volgograd]. You could say I experienced the war in both countries. I heard what the Germans were told over the German radio, and here I experienced air raids and suchlike. It was a rather unique experience that I had, as it were, in double vision or stereoscopically. It did not fill me with joy. I could not rejoice when German cities were bombed, of course not. But it had to be, and that's how it was.

In 1945 it would have been theoretically possible to return to my native country, but what would we have lived on? The principal fact was that here I had a livelihood and a son who was born English. Reemigration was not really an option. For me it was a matter of course that I would return to the Warburg Institute. My parents and my sisters were in England, and to return suddenly to a shattered Vienna was impossible. I received a rather lukewarm letter from the Albertina library, asking if I was thinking of a possible return, but that wasn't a real offer.

Later, Austria awarded me all kinds of orders — the Austrian Cross of Honor and the Austrian Mark of Honor, the Wittgenstein Prize and the Culture Prize of the City of Vienna; I was made an honorary member of the Austrian Art Historians' Union — all this pleases me, naturally. But I always say my case should not be generalized. There has always been and there still is what has been called the republic of letters. We scientists and scholars, the *res publica literarum* belong together and are domiciled in our work. I don't feel I am English; I feel precisely what I am — a Central European working in England. Thanks to my work at the BBC I learned English thoroughly. This work really was an enormous factor: If throughout six years you translate German into English for eight hours a day, you really come to know the language. As a result, people say that I write good English. After all, I received the Order of Merit here, the highest distinction.

It is important, however, to remember that we are untypical cases. One should never, never forget that a lot of people had a terribly bad time because it was so difficult to get a work permit. A whole lot of highly gifted people came here as domestic staff. A popular opportunity was employment as a "married couple," the husband as butler and the wife as cook. It so happens that I had recently something to do with the story of the outstanding Austrian painter Gerhart Frankl; he escaped from the Nazis in this way. Some people were very considerate, but others believed that once they'd given them employment these people should also work accordingly. My father was quite unusual in this respect. As I have said, he used to be an attorney, but he immediately resolved to work here in some way or other. The firm of removal agents who transported our furniture and our piano to England gave him a job because he could speak German. Although he was a poor one-finger typist, he immediately went there as an office worker. He had no false pride at all. My mother, of course, found it easier to earn money, which was one more reason for him to want to earn as well. Gradually he learned to type better, and while we were living in Oxford, he typed doctoral theses. He didn't want to be kept by his wife.

People often believe that ours was an "expulsion to Paradise," as Erwin Panofsky once said in America. He had a wonderful time; he went straight to the Institute of Art at Princeton. But for most people it was anything but paradise. They had first to learn English; they were hardly able to express themselves. They first learned all the customs, all the things that are a matter of course here, how to light a fire in an open fireplace — all that had to be learned first.

Marianne Erdfarb
Bronx, New York

Marianne Erdfarb, born as Marianne Katz on April 10, 1926, in Vienna; 5 years primary school (Grünergasse, 9th District); entered Schwarzwaldschule Realgymnasium (Wallnerstrasse, Vienna 1) in 1936. Banned from school attendance at the end of the 1937-38 academic year; passed entrance examination to Chajes Realgymnasium (20th District). Attended third form until July 1939, then escaped from Vienna on October 18, 1939. Arrived in New York on November 4, 1939. After graduation from American high school trained as a grade school teacher; worked in education until July 1991. Married, 1947; three sons (born 1949, 1953, and 1956), ten grandchildren.

The reason I have not been to Vienna again is quite simply that the Viennese have kicked me out, and all my feelings for that city or for Austria have been totally driven out of me. I didn't want to see another German face. The *New York Times* had a few articles recently about Vienna, and I read them all. Two years ago I had the book *Das jüdische Wien* ["Jewish Vienna"] sent to me and I read it. But that is all. I also read everything about Waldheim. I wouldn't have thought he'd become federal president of Austria. I was greatly surprised they didn't know anything about these matters in the United Nations. Only after the newspaper disclosures did they discover that he'd been with the Nazis, and I think this is a sordid business. But even without the Waldheim affair I would never want to return to Austria — not once.

My children know everything — what happened to my parents and grandparents. My grandfather is buried at the Vienna Zentralfriedhof. He was a soldier in the First World War. My step-grandfather committed suicide on October 31, 1938. When on November 10 the Nazis arrived in order to deport him to Dachau, he was already dead. They actually said, "Such underhandedness! When we try to pick up some Jews, they're all dead already!" Instead they picked up my father and took him to Dachau. He got out on January 17, 1939, probably because our aunt managed to get us visas for Nicaragua and Costa Rica in Italy. We bought our tickets for the passage, and everything was arranged for our emigration. And when he got home on January 17, Nicaragua and Costa Rica had declared they weren't accepting any more Jews.

We were lucky: Our quota number for America was sent to us in August 1939. We landed here on November 4, 1939. My paternal grandparents had arrived before us because my grandfather had attended his brother's wedding here in 1890. And because he'd been in the U.S. once before, he was given a quota number immediately. So we first moved in with our grandparents. I was very, very happy to be in America. To me America had been a dreamland where the streets were paved with money. My grandparents looked after us and things weren't too bad. My father had seven cousins, and every one of them came to visit us. We arrived on a Saturday, and on Sunday they all came to see us and each gave us $5. Thus my father had $35 and felt really rich. My cousin Robert Katz had come over in July 1939. His parents had been afraid that he'd be arrested; they were born in Poland, but he was a Viennese. People from Vienna were able to travel then, and so they sent him over.

Thus, when the three of us arrived in the States, we lived in one room, and my grandparents and cousin in another. There were three people to a bed, so at first we were in tight circumstances. My father — he often told the story — earned his first 50¢ by helping a man push a push-cart up a hill. Later he found work as a tailor. It was very difficult for my parents, but they were happy to be in America and no longer in Austria.

Why was this so? Because over the preceding eighteen months we had been through too much in Austria. When one is so humiliated, when one is deprived of all rights, this remains engraved on one's memory. As for myself, I got into an American school after a week. I was only 13, and you had to be 14 to get into high school. But my cousin, who was a little older than me, quite simply took me along to his high school and said if we could speak English we were old enough to go to high school. So that's what happened. A lot can be done in the U.S.A. in an unbureaucratic way that would have been impossible in Vienna. I had been taught English in the third form in Vienna, but it was only for 77 days in the whole of the

1938-39 academic year, and of course I couldn't speak much English. In my first week at school they gave me an English grammar test and I got 96 out of a possible 100. We had to underline the subject and the predicate, and that I could do. I knew Latin, German, a little Italian, a little English and a little Hebrew. In all those languages I knew what the subject and the predicate were. The teacher asked me if I had copied, but in fact the other children had copied from me; this I shall never forget. She put me next to another child who spoke Yiddish, and I couldn't speak Yiddish. That wasn't very clever, but somehow I learned English.

In Vienna I'd had six and a half years of schooling. Here in America they took my school reports and sent them to Albany, the capital of New York, and for those six and a half years they credited me with nine years because of my good Austrian schooling. That was the reputation Austrian education enjoyed. In November I entered the first grade, and in February they moved me up to third grade. From third grade I moved into fifth grade, and from the fifth to seventh. In seventh grade they kept me for two years because of the important preparation for graduation, then they moved me up into eighth. At 16 I graduated. In point of fact, I had always been good at school. Once a good student, always a good student, and perhaps it isn't surprising that I became a teacher. At my secondary school in Vienna, the teachers were good colleagues — more friends then teachers. As a result I was good at school. Nowadays here in New York you can no longer be a friend to the students. It is not possible to apply the good Austrian educational system, of which I was a product, here in America. That they just don't know how to do. We had a teachers' conference recently, and the principal instructed us, "You must never touch a child! If you touch them the parents can sue you, and you could be expelled from the school!" You're not allowed to touch a child, not even put a reassuring arm on their shoulders.

My father was in Dachau from November 10 to January 17. He told me that when he was taken there by train, he had to sit with his hands at his side and look into the lamp all the time — just a piece of chicanery the guards had thought up. He never received any compensation for what he went through at Dachau. My mother later received about $1,000 and some additional sums in dollars for the shop they'd taken from her in Austria. But that was all — no one in the family received any other compensation. But that has nothing to do with the fact that I am so bitter about Austria. I was bitter about what Hitler — after all, he was an Austrian — had done to the Jewish people there.

Could Austria have done anything to make us forgive the injustice done to us? I don't think so. I believe that there is nothing Austria could have done to make forgiveness easier for us. I said to myself, I don't want ever to see any Germans or Austrians again. They expelled me, and I will not go back. I had to leave, and I have no reason to return.

The sound of heavy boots still makes me nervous, simply from the memory of that day. I think it was about five in the morning. Our flat had windows giving on the passage. The Gestapo men knocked on the window, and their jackboots made an infernal racket in the passage. These sounds have become unbearable for me. To this day, if somebody raps on the table I get frantically nervous. Whenever that happens I am reminded of the day when the Nazis came, rapped on the door and burst into our apartment. First they looked for my grandfather, and, because they could no longer kill him, they took my father away with them. I no longer have nightmares now as I used to. The terrible thing is that I don't feel secure in this country either. When I came to America, things were fine here, the best country in the world. Now there is much more anti–Semitism in America than there used to be, and I'm scared. I can't get rid of the idea that when I go to a park or to a movie theater somebody might come along and yell, "Jews out!" This goes back to Vienna, where, after the Anschluss, notices were fixed to all benches in the park: "Prohibited to Jews." And in the movie theaters it was "Jews out!" This is still lodged in my head, and I don't suppose it'll go away as long as I live.

Anny Robert
Tel Aviv

Anny Robert, born as Anny Marcus on July 31, 1909, in Vienna. Attended primary and lower secondary schools in Vienna, then two years at a dressmaking academy in Michelbeuerngasse; gained three years practical experience in a Vienna salon and subsequently found independent work. Active member of Social Democratic Party. Because of political threat in 1935, escaped from Austro-fascism to Palestine. Survived difficult years with dressmaking and occasional work. Married an Austrian refugee, later divorced. Battled serious illness; retired in 1969. In Israel she began to write poems, some of them published also in Austria. Has given numerous readings, largely in senior citizens' clubs.

━━━━━━━━━━━━━

In Israel one always tells visitors that one is happy here, that Israel is the only true home. I am an individualist, and I can't say this is true of me. I would be lying. We have always been more or less independent; we had to work our way up, which we did, but that I immediately felt happy here — no. The fact that after so many years I got a divorce is a different subject. I suffered badly from something — I didn't really know from what. I read a great deal and concerned myself a lot with Freud. After many years, when I was in a deep depression, a doctor told me: "In your case the diagnosis is easy — you are deracinated!" I never wanted to admit to myself that I was homesick, but I don't think it's a sin to admit to homesickness. But I'd had to suppress this homesickness continually because my husband — while he was here — immediately swung round, although in Austria he'd never been a Zionist. And when I began to talk about it, he'd say, "Well then, go back to Hitler!" What was I to answer to that? Of course I was very thankful that I didn't have to experience the years after 1938 there, and my nostalgia then abated a little. But in fairly mature years I had a serious operation. Thinking about it today I believe that it was an escape into illness. And after 33 years here I was at last able to fulfill my greatest wish — to see Vienna once more.

I want to be correctly understood. I am grateful to fate that we got here so early and didn't have to experience everything on our own skins. Of course, we shared the experience because a large part of my family lost their lives, but we experienced it from a distance. Body and soul hang together. And with my reason I have told myself a hundred times: This now is your homeland. And yet, that sense of home which I felt for Vienna — I never felt that sense of home again for Israel. I keep emphasizing: I am glad I am here; at my age a return would be out of the question. In 1985 I was invited to Austria, along with a small group. Before then I'd been to Austria altogether five times, and once in England for a couple of weeks. And I must say I didn't feel any anti–Semitism, though I always said at once that I was coming from Israel, if only to avoid unpleasant surprises.

What do I long for, in particular? Specific things that exist in Vienna and which have absolutely nothing to do with people — the Viennese air, the special atmosphere of Vienna. Just as everything gets weaker with age, so my longing for Austria has also become weaker — certainly since I've been in a home here. But maybe this is just because I know with complete certainty that I cannot afford a trip abroad either on health grounds or financially. This sense of home that I had for Vienna — for instance, when I returned from a skiing trip or whenever my heart started throbbing in my throat the moment we got to Heiligenstatt, when I caught sight of the first red tramcar. Perhaps I've inherited this; my father was like that too.

Thank God my father died in 1936, so he was spared the worst. Which unfortunately was not the case with my mother. We couldn't get her out because we were here illegally. We had no certificate, so we could not apply for her release; she was deported to Theresienstadt (Terezín), as were some other members of my family. I'm ambivalent now. Of course, if I were well enough and could afford to visit Vienna once more for two or three weeks… And that time, five years ago, the one week was very enjoyable. But I must point out that after this one week I was glad to get back here to this home. One's got to be grateful for everything.

I've been writing poems for many years, and some of them have been published, in Austria and here. One of them is called "Prayer":

If I had my life once more
would I want money galore?
Would I want a lot of kids?
Would I live just by my wits?
Would I want to be a whore?
Would a nun's life suit me more?
Be a tumbler at a fair?
Would I like to have red hair?
To such questions every day
I have only this to say:
Dear God, if it be your pleasure
to grant me another measure
of this earthly life, yes then
let me be the same again!
If you made me brave and strong
something else would have gone wrong.
Let me therefore all I've done
do again on my next run.
Let me love and let me bitch,
sometimes poor and sometimes rich.
Let me feel and let me live,
let me take and let me give;
let me laugh and let me cry,
let the sun shine from the sky!
Let the rain fall on my hair,
let me bless and let me swear,
let me pray and let me kiss,
let me hear and let me know,
let me write and let me sew.
Leave me my long working hours
and my seconds of pure bliss!
Lord, I thank you in advance.
Only one thing let me ask,
Lord, it's not an easy task:
Going down right to the roots,
could you change the attitudes
of the races you created,
so that they no longer hated
one another? Be so good:
leave me where my cradle stood.
Even on some distant strand,
even, say, on Helgoland.
Let me sweat and let me freeze
but do not displace me, please!
Spare me, if you will, one fate —
do not make me
emigrate!

People whose children were born here, which unfortunately was not granted to me, are much more linked to this country — because it is their children's home. Even though ultimately your home is where you were born. Of course I am pro–Israel, that's what my head tells me. And I am not entirely unfeeling — but it is something like a marriage of convenience.

Paul Selkowitsch
New York

Paul Selkowitsch, born August 5, 1913, in Vienna into a Viennese working class family. Attended primary and lower secondary schools and undertook a commercial apprenticeship specializing on window dressing. After his father's deportation to Dachau in April 1938, escaped to Czechoslovakia, having to leave his mother behind. With the help of Czech Social Democrats, escaped to Palestine down the Danube. In Palestine, worked as an orange picker and sign writer. After the war, married. Wife died at the birth of their first child; soon afterward the child died. Served with the Israeli air force during the War of Liberation. Married a second time in 1949; a few years later, immigrated (with his wife) to the U.S. Now running a successful transportation business here. His brother is the writer Herbert Selkowitsch.

I was born in 1913. My parents were also born in Vienna, and so were my maternal grandparents. Alfred Adler, the famous individual psychologist, was my cousin. As far as anti–Semitism is concerned, I didn't have any bad experiences in Austria until the Anschluss. I was never called a "Yid" or anything of the kind by anybody.

Under Dollfuss I was active in the underground Social Democratic party. I used to deliver the *Arbeiterzeitung*,[10] which was printed in Switzerland on tissue paper and sent to Austria, from house to house.

I got to Israel illegally. I first went to Brno, in Czechoslovakia, and there the League for Human Rights looked after me. The Socialist International then had an office there for the support of former underground socialists. As I was such a one, they helped me with a monthly subsidy. And then they secured for me a place on a ship to Israel, then Palestine.

We were 500 or 600 people on that ship, which was designed for something like half that number. It was an illegal transport; earlier it had carried arms supplies to the Spanish Reds. We were all of us sick. We had been given sausages by the Jewish community in Romania, which had evidently made us all ill. We had one dead, whom we threw overboard into the sea. We came to Israel under terrible conditions, first on the Danube and then at sea. And we were permanently on the alert for British vessels; these would have shipped us back. Those English humanists actually sent the people they caught back to Germany and Austria! Thank God we arrived at Nathania, where the Jewish population took us in: They gave us clothes, they fed us, and we were able to bathe.

So we were in Palestine. There, overnight, I became a peasant. I had no clue at all about farm work, but this was the only way I could keep alive. My first wife was with me; she was pregnant at the time. We had a daughter, who unfortunately died of severe stomach and intestinal poisoning. And my wife also died of poisoning, in mental confusion. Her blood had got mixed with her milk, and she had no idea then who she was or who I was. She died in frightful circumstances. That was in 1939, shortly after our arrival in Palestine.

As I said, I worked in the fields, I picked oranges, and I dug the earth with a spade. It wasn't work I was used to, but I did it gladly. Later I kept myself by other work, by sign writing. I was rather successful with this, and I had quite a few customers for whom I made signs to order.

In Israel I met my second wife. I was in the air force. She had miscarried three times, and, as the doctor was worried about her, she was not allowed to become pregnant again, and so we remained childless. After all these experiences in Israel, when I'd been in the forces and on permanent alert, we decided to go to America. Our friends there sent us an affidavit. That was after the Sinai War. We arrived in America in 1957, each of us with $10 in our pockets — no question of rebuilding our lives. But friends helped me, rented an apartment and paid the rent for months on end. Then I found a job and my wife worked in a factory. Thus we gradually acclimatized. Now we've been here for 31 years and, thank God, cannot complain. We've made it, as the saying goes; we're not rich, but we have enough to live on.

I am already a little homesick for Austria. But after all that has happened, after all the bestialities I've heard about, after those brutal events — and the Austrians were worse and more fanatical than the Germans — I told myself, No! I couldn't live there any more. And one gets ever new proof of this. In 1966 we were in Salzburg for the festival, and we went to a restaurant. We were the only guests except for four men at a table some distance away. They were drinking beer. They evidently noticed or suspected that we were Jews. Anyway, they began a loud conversation, something like: "Oh yes, the Jews in America, they had it in for us! That Rosenfeld [this is what they called Roosevelt] was just such a Jew!" Which, of course, is absolutely untrue. "And Hitler was quite right: the Jews and the Jews and the Jews…" Then the waitress came to us and apologized. "That is not the mood here in Salzburg," she said. I said, "There's nothing to apologize for. Let me have my bill and we'll leave!" Of course we felt sick. I would have liked to argue with those people, but thought better of it because of my temperament: I would have got into a brawl, and it would have come to a bad end.

I have been to Vienna nearly every year because my parents used to live there. I had no bad reactions, except that I felt that everybody I met had once been a Nazi. And this feeling marred my pleasure at being in Austria. And then there was that episode in Salzburg — that was probably the climax. My school used to be in Weintraubengasse, but it is no longer there. Across the street from it there is now a brothel. I went to where we used to live, on Praterstrasse; there was the Hauswirt restaurant, one of the most famous in Vienna. I once went there on my own for lunch. Of course the old owner is no longer alive. I also went to the house where we used to live, to our floor, and there I had sense of great loss. Of all that we lost. We were the only tenants. Now the house is gone, they pulled it down a few years later. There's just an empty space.

Walter Foster
London

Walter Foster, born as Walter Fast on June 25, 1923, in Vienna. Attended primary school and Realgymnasium in Vienna. Escaped from Austria on December 17, 1938; after a brief period at the South East Technical College in Dagenham, England, interned as an "enemy alien" in May 1940 and was deported to Australia; volunteered for the British army in Australia. Returned to England at the beginning of 1942; first in the Pioneer Corps, subsequently in the Royal Electrical and Mechanical Engineers until 1946. From 1946 to 1950, worked as a fitter, joiner and building contractor. Married in 1948 and had four children. Since 1950, has worked in the management of the Anglo-Austrian Society; from 1959 until 1992, as its secretary-general. Conducted repeated negotiations between Britain and Austria: student exchanges, travel arrangements, language classes, all kinds of cultural events. Has received several distinctions from the Austrian Republic.

I was born Walter Fast in Vienna in 1923. I chose the name Foster when I was serving in the British army — because, if the Germans had taken me prisoner, my old surname would have meant instant death. After the so-called Kristallnacht — a term I have never gotten used to — my mother managed to get me on a children's transport to England. That was on December 17, 1938. On December 18, I arrived here from Holland and was first taken to Dovercourt, which was a reception camp for refugee children. Dovercourt was owned by a holiday camp company. When Easter came along, they needed the camp again for their visitors, and most of us soon disappeared from there — the blue-eyed fair-curled little girls first, then the other pretty children, and the teenage boys whom nobody wanted

148

were left. And unfortunately I was one of the latter. Next we were accommodated at a farmhouse near Ipswich, and from there we eventually came to a home run by a small Jewish community on the outskirts of London, in Beacontree, between Ilford and Dagenham. There were four boys of my age, fifteen to sixteen years old, three Germans and I, and the local rabbi. We were looked after by a German refugee lady. After a break of several weeks, I went to school again because we weren't allowed to work.

In the war we had to face so-called "aliens' tribunals"—executive committees which had to determine how dangerous we were. There were three categories: Category C, "friendly enemy aliens"—a paradox that didn't seem to anybody as funny; Category A, the damnable ones, potential enemies of the state, who were immediately interned; and in between, Group B, to which I was assigned. I never managed to discover why, but rumor had it that it was because the Bloomsbury House refugee organization had an agreement with the aliens' tribunals to the effect that boys of my age shouldn't be allowed to roam about the country too freely. Hence they had restrictions imposed on them. If one belonged to Category B, one was not permitted to leave the London region or stay away overnight. And because I was in Category B, I was interned in May 1940 after the British withdrawal from Dunkirk, while the Category C people were not interned until June or July. I was able to collect a lot of experience about internment—first I was on a racecourse at Long Kempton Park; then in Huyton internment camp, where nearly everybody was at some time or other; then on the Isle of Man, at a place called Onchan, where family hotels were cleared out and surrounded with barbed wire. And there we sat in these empty houses and received rations which, as far as I recall, consisted mainly of salted herrings and oat flakes, from which we were supposed to cook something, never mind what. That was uncomfortable but amusing; there were a lot of educated people there. I made the acquaintance there of a whole series of eminent artists, politicians and scientists. But things were getting more and more disagreeable the nearer the German armored divisions got to the Channel Coast. We were guarded by elderly Home Guard men, who were neither dangerous nor unpleasant. But one worried all the time whether the next morning they wouldn't be relieved by the SS.

It then became known in the camps that the internees were to be shipped overseas, to Canada. We didn't know why, but I found the thought that one might avoid possible capture by the SS by putting an ocean instead of just a channel between them and us not unattractive. Besides, considerable moral pressure was applied to young people like myself. Why?

Because older people did not want to be shipped overseas, as they had wives and children in London or wherever who had not been interned. We youngsters, who had nothing to lose, were to volunteer so the older ones could stay near their families. So it came to pass that one day I found myself on board the *Dunera*. After a foot march from the Isle of Man, we were taken by a small ship to Fleetwood, and thence by rail to Liverpool. There we marched from the station to the port — through excited crowds who reviled us as German prisoners and now and again pelted us with rotten apples and suchlike. It was not pleasant, as a decisive opponent of Nazism, to be reviled as a Nazi; it seemed a monstrous injustice. And then the *Dunera*, an interesting ship that was to go down in history. It was all hemmed with barbed wire — if it had sunk no one would have gotten away. The front of the ship was separated from the rear; we were divided into two groups and we didn't know who was in the other part of the ship. We never met. On board our guard consisted of people who had committed some offense on the retreat from France, and instead of putting them into prison at a time of manpower shortage they were posted as a guard crew on a prison ship. They behaved accordingly. We were not only treated most rudely, but we were also robbed and maltreated. Nothing can character-ize the situation better than the fact that the commanding officer, a British army colonel, was court-martialed as soon as the ship arrived, and sen-tenced to two years imprisonment for neglect of duty.[11]

The voyage to Canada proceeded laboriously. We were allegedly tor-pedoed on our way; we heard a crash but we didn't sink. At times it was terribly rough, and for the only time in my life I was really seasick. I reflected that I couldn't afford to be seasick, for if the ship was sunk I'd have to be able to swim. Then the sun rose higher and higher in the sky, and when in a palm-fringed port small tenders were approaching our ship, there was no doubt left that we were not being taken to Canada. It was Cape Town, and a few weeks later we continued across the Indian Ocean to Australia. The whole business took eight weeks. The *Dunera*, moreover, also carried the survivors of the *Arandora Star*; these included crews of real German ships, genuine Nazi sailors. The *Arandora Star* was a ship that had attempted the voyage to Canada before the *Dunera*; she mainly carried Italian internees as well as a few German prisoners of war. The ship was torpedoed and sank, and it is not accurately known how many people were on board.[12] A small portion of them were saved, and some 300 or 400 were put on board the *Dunera*. Very considerate, wasn't it? The Italians were mostly elderly people who had worked all their lives as waiters in Italian restaurants in London, but in England, too, they held that "a regulation is a regulation," and so these poor blighters were arrested. The Germans, as I've said, were real Nazi sailors, who behaved entirely correctly toward us, except that they chose the quarters from which it would be easiest to escape in case the ship sank. Of course they knew best how to get out of a ship surrounded by barbed wire. It suited us all right, because we knew that they'd have no time to close the gap after them and we'd be able to get out too.

In Australia we were again interned. When we asked where we were being taken they made a vague gesture toward the west. Some 500 miles west of Sydney was the camp, in surroundings that the Australians call the bush and others call the desert. There we were interned in two separate camps, at Hay. The Australians soon discovered that there had been a terrible misunderstanding, because they had expected German prisoners of war and not people like us. So they said, "Know what? This barbed wire circle in the bush is a piece of England, for which the British government is responsible, let them deal with it. You can have anything to eat you like; you can do what you like." And we really got any food we wished.

Through the Jewish community in Sydney, they then obtained books for us and we had a wonderful library. We organized a camp university, where first-rate experts lectured on any subject we chose. Meat rations were enormous, too much to handle. They were so large that after a few months I joined a vegetarian group, because vegetables were also available in any quantities, likewise fruit. The meat was mainly mutton, which for me, as a Central European, was most unusual at that time. Mutton was something they ate in the Balkans, but a Viennese or a German of course didn't eat mutton. So we used the mutton, or rather the mutton fat, for other purposes; we had excellent chemists with us for whom it was no problem to make soap from it. I learned a lot there. Among other things, I was the camp postmaster, I learned how to print money (not real money, but camp money) and how one cuts a stamp and uses it for printing. In another camp I became a carpenter's apprentice with a chemist — prior to Hitler an assistant professor at Vienna University — whose hobby was fine cabinetmaking. And never in my life, either before or since, did I read so many and such good books; I never had so much time again. One had an infinite amount of time there; that was the worst of it.

That whole joke in Australia lasted long enough. We'd left England at the beginning of July and arrived in Australia in September. So I made my first attempt to get away from Australia by volunteering for the British army. Thereupon I was sent to the fifth or sixth camp of my internment history — at a place called Liverpool, near Sydney, where we waited for a suitable ship. And while we were in Liverpool the Pearl Harbor business happened, on December 7, a great date in American history. And after that, of course, nothing happened at all for several weeks, until January 1942. No one knew where the Japanese navy was. Therefore we still had the status of prisoners on the ship on which we traveled. No one was prepared to release us. On board there were not only a few Jews from Vienna or Germany, but also a complete crew of Australian sailors who had to be taken to Britain to take over a destroyer. Like ourselves they were condemned to twiddling their thumbs. Also on board was a cargo of Norwegian sailors whose ship had been sunk. But the most important cargo was the last cargo of tin, got out from Malaysia before it was overrun by the Japanese. The Australians gave us an escort of two real cruisers as far as New Zealand; off the New Zealand coast they about-turned and sailed back to Australia, because Australia had to be defended against the Japanese. We were now to be the responsibility of the New Zealanders. From New Zealand we sailed down almost to the Antarctic, to avoid Japanese torpedoes, and up the South American coast, through the Panama Canal and via Bermuda to Canada.

So I got to Canada after all. There we froze miserably for ten days in the Port of Halifax — I had never been so cold in my life. We were waiting for a convoy. That convoy never materialized, except for two ships: The one with the last cargo of tin and the sailors and a Dutch ship which in peacetime had been a luxury transatlantic liner. The liner carried the first American division going to Europe. Two exceedingly important ships, therefore, because of the tin and because of the Americans. The Germans probably knew what was in those ships — their secret service operated efficiently in the States. Anyway, we set out from Halifax at the beginning of February 1942, and throughout the crossing of the Atlantic, the two ships were continually fired on. That was the time when I came closest to the war, when one was under fire day and night. It was one of the grandest and most eerie experiences of my life. The two ships, because they were fast, were escorted by two destroyers of the British navy — four vessels in all, which had to rely on their speed rather than on protection. A German U-boat fired torpedoes on the ship with the Americans, one could see the torpedoes, and one of the destroyers interposed itself and, as it were, intercepted the torpedoes with its body. The British navy could not afford to have the first U.S. troopship under its protection to be sunk. Nothing was left of the destroyer, nothing at all. The rest, of course, had to sail on as fast as possible, so there was no time to look for survivors.

When I got back to England they had, in typically British manner, lost my papers, and although in theory I was already in the British army, they sent me back to the Isle of Man to be on the safe side, until they found my papers. Then I found myself in the British army, next to the Huyton internment camp, converted meanwhile into a training camp for the Pioneer Corps. They only allowed us into the Pioneer Corps, the men with a spade instead of a rifle. There I recovered for a while in a hospital from the cold which I had presumably caught in the Port of Halifax after coming from the tropics. Eventually I found myself in 251 Company, Pioneer Corps. That was in Bicester, near Oxford, where we chiefly dug trenches and built hutments, standing waist-deep in mud — simple, honest and healthy work. The worst thing in the Pioneer Corps was not the discipline nor the work, but the boredom. I volunteered for all kinds of adventurous enterprises, but chance had it that I was not accepted anywhere — luckily, I suppose, because otherwise I probably wouldn't be alive.

I concluded my military career after the war during the occupation of Germany as an interpreter with the military government in Westphalia, where they simultaneously employed me as a de facto inspector of prisons. One saw a lot of awful things in Germany then — Germany, of course, was totally devastated. When I eventually succeeded in getting out of the army, I wanted to use the opportunity for a quick visit to Vienna. I made out my own pass because my commanding officer didn't want an Austrian to go to Vienna, and so I traveled as a British soldier — an adventurous business but not very important. That was in 1946.

When I was first marching into Germany with my unit, if I may put it that way, I thought, "these terrible Germans — and the crimes they committed!" You arrived with a tommy gun in your hand and thought you'd go *bang-bang!*, but this was not what happened at all. The first thing we did was to screen out the big Nazis from the small ones, the war criminals from the fellow travelers. This whole screening business — I could write books about it. The most important detail was that anyone below a senior rank, anyone below major, at least, and anyone less than 35 was not even looked at; they were sent home. We said, "These are too young, too stupid; they were not in a key position — send them home!" For that reason First Lieutenant Waldheim would have been of no interest whatever to me.

We'd have automatically sent him home, and nobody would have cared what he'd done.

On this first visit to Austria I looked up several people, found them again, and talked to them. I only found a single Jew who had survived in Vienna — a fellow student who had been a friend. I spotted his name on a list; to me he was just a boy at the next desk, with whom I swapped Latin words. He survived because his piano teacher, a woman, hid him in a cupboard, throughout four years. And whenever anyone says something against Austria and the Viennese, I remember Paul and his piano teacher. He couldn't have lived from the teacher's ration cards, so at least half a dozen other people must have known about him and been prepared to sacrifice something of their own rations so he might have something to eat in his cupboard. There he was from the time when the deportations to Poland started to the day when the Russians arrived. He was traumatized, naturally; but, astonishingly, he resumed his studies at the Technical University, graduated as a mechanical engineer, and eventually immigrated to America.

There were people who lost one homeland and never found another — but that was not my case. I did not lose my native country. I have always retained my relationship with Austria. My country was temporarily — if one may call the Hitler years temporary — barred to me. I knew what was happening in Austria to the extent that I could get hold of information. It was pretty obvious to me what was happening; I understood the connections. I had no illusions, no particular love relationship, but a realistic attitude, a belief that somehow I belonged there. "For better or worse," as they say here; I simply belong. But in my generation I don't know anyone else — I consider myself atypical — who has kept up a real relationship with Austria. As for the question of collective guilt, I soon answered that for myself. I thought, if I hadn't happened to be a Jew I might have been that first lieutenant in the Balkans, and I don't wish to claim that I would have behaved differently from Waldheim. That's why I don't condemn him, because that would be condemning myself and all my colleagues from school. It was mere chance that I wasn't one of them. Who knows, perhaps I would have been a good Nazi. I can't swear to it; maybe I would have been a Resistance hero. The most probable thing is that I would have kept my mouth shut and run with the rest, just as the others did.

Richard Berczeller

New York

Richard Berczeller, born February 4, 1902, in Ödenburg (now Sopron, Hungary). His father was the founder of the Social Democratic Party in German Western Hungary and its first representative in Hungary.[13] Attended schools in Ödenburg; studied medicine in Vienna and took his degree in 1926. From 1926 to 1930 received hospital training and worked as personnel officer of physicians at the municipal hospitals under Julius Tandler. From 1930 to 1938, had a medical practice in Mattersburg. Arrested by the Gestapo. Released with assistance from Anna Freud. Escaped to Paris; served as colonial doctor in the then–French colony of the Ivory Coast. Owing to sickness, returned to Paris; in 1940, escaped to southern France with his wife and six-year-old son. Immigrated to U.S. and arrived in New York, 1941; after language examination and catching up on medical studies, became a general practitioner in New York. Beginning in 1963, enjoyed a successful career as an author: *Displaced Doctor*; *Time Was*; *Mit Österreich verbunden* [*Linked to Austria*] (jointly with Norbert Leser); *A Trip Into the Blue and Other Stories from the New Yorker*; *Zeitgeschichte in Konfrontationen* [*Modern History in Confrontations*] (jointly with Norbert Leser). Wrote numerous articles (*Aufbau*; *AZ*; *Zukunft*; *The New Yorker*). Richard Berczeller died on January 3, 1994, at age 91.

New York to me is the prototype of an exile city. Everybody was assembled here in New York — the Zernatto group was there,[14] Otto von Habsburg was there, there was a group I belonged to, and then there was Buttinger. These groups didn't get on with each other at all. We middle-class people held totally different views from the Habsburg crowd. Although I was the doctor of many of them, I never really behaved aggressively toward them, but in line with my nature, got on with those people, even though I made no ideological concessions. Nevertheless we had a serious argument, especially on the issue of the Austrian battalion that Otto von Habsburg wanted to establish. I should point out, however, that I never belonged to the ideological first division. For that I lacked the necessary education. My father played a far more important role back home as a Social Democrat than I did.

But, to be perfectly honest, I knew everybody. I participated everywhere. Also in the American phase of our emigration. And I was not only a doctor in emigration; I later also became an author. I am a member of the American PEN [Association of Poets, Playwrights, Editors, Essayists and Novelists], but never engaged in association politics with them. I was friendly with Waldinger; I was even virtually related to him because Waldinger married a niece of Freud, and my wife is the confidante of the family. He was a highly gifted person, really a wonderful colleague, and I am very sorry that he is no longer known in Austria. With regard to Alfred Polgar, the following happened: I was in southern France when Pétain was in power, and thus the whole of southern France was turned into a part of fascist France. And one day a couple come to me and introduce themselves as Polgar. I hadn't known him personally before. And he said, "Doctor, I've come to see you because my wife and I want to commit suicide. I would like you to give me some poison!" This is the first time I've told this to anyone. The Germans were getting ever closer, and people were afraid. So I said to him, "Listen, why not wait a little longer? If the Germans get here, and if I'm still about, then we'll do it." That was at Montauban, not far from Toulouse. I never saw him again; I had no personal relationship with him. But at least I can take credit for the fact that he didn't commit suicide. Whom else did I know? Well, the Austrians didn't have any really prominent people here. Yes, there was Stefan Zweig; he was here for a short time. I knew his wife, Friederike, very well. She died here, and she came from here. She often sent word that she'd like to see me, but she couldn't get to New York. I kept postponing our meeting, until she died. Most of the people were unlucky, not Stefan Zweig, but for instance Max Reinhardt; he never made it here, nor did Franz Molnar.[15]

As for how the refugees felt toward Austria, I described that in numerous lectures, letters, and books. In intelligent people, there was a dichotomy between head and heart. The head was against collective guilt and argued politically, ideologically in the whole business. But the heart experienced it all quite differently. I was a country doctor, treating socialists, clericals, Jews and Christians all alike—and one day they came, arrested me, and put me in jail. We were beaten, our apartment was ransacked and everything we still had was carted off. We were three brothers—the youngest was murdered. Before the Anschluss, he had shared a cell with Bruno Kreisky, the postwar chancellor. Thus, when you were kicked out into exile, when you had to struggle through France, when you were a doctor in Africa, and when you had to start from scratch again in America, then of course, on emotional grounds, you reject a return. One wanted to integrate. And one said to oneself, "Thank God I found a livelihood again. What's more, a better one than the one I had in the past—so the Austrians can take a running jump."

Anyway, I am one of the very few they invited back. I flew there and had a look. I liked what I saw. I could have had a fairly high position— head of the Vienna District Health Service and eventually a deputy in the Burgenland provincial parliament. But by then my son was a medical student and it was difficult. Practical considerations played a part—the fact that here in America I am a U.S. citizen now, that I have security here and a different atmosphere, even though there is a good deal of reaction, as well as difficulties and slovenliness. I actually once demonstrated in a speech that America is a land of unlimited *impossibilities.* As time passed I thought more and more often, "Why on earth should I leave this country?" Even so, I have not become an American.

The people who felt happy with their livelihood here naturally said, "Here we are, here we stay." Here was security. When a person has been here for ten, twenty, thirty years, then he'll end up saying, "Here we are, here we stay." Whether, nevertheless, they felt unhappy, or whether they complained that the coffee or the service wasn't good? Certainly at first. Especially the Austrians, who are fond of complaining—it's a national characteristic. That has always existed. But there hasn't been any violent yearning to return. People who thought politically, who acted politically, had less nostalgia. Certainly Max Reinhardt, whom I didn't know personally, would have longed to be back at his chateau of Leopoldskron near Salzburg. Or Franz Molnar, who is a patient of mine, he certainly yearned to go back. Waldinger certainly, although he had difficulties, he was a very strongly Austrian-oriented person.[16] For some people culture and cultural work played a major part. That is why I mentioned the conflict between head and heart. Of course they said what happened to us was monstrous; but ultimately it is as I said: A man can have many homes but only one homeland—putting it a little bombastically. Do I still have something like a sense of homeland? To be frank, there is some nostalgia. But I am an exceptional case. Exceptional because I knew people there, people among the revolutionary socialists, who made sacrifices, and because I knew that there was also another Austria, and that Austrian opportunism is as great as anywhere in the world. I have tried to rationalize this, which means I am talking about the head. The emotional aspect is more like a dream vision.

Ours is an entirely Austrian household. All our Austrian visitors say that this is the most Austrian house in America. My wife still cooks Austrian cuisine, just as she did in Africa. Here you can eat the best schnitzel and the best gugelhupf; for me it is still "at my place in Austria"—and with that I'll die. You can't give up emotional values. I was born in Ödenburg. Even as quite a young boy I was in prison after the Horthy business, and I suffered for my country and social democracy at an early age.[17] And I longed terribly for my home, for years and decades; it is a recurrent dream. In my dream there is, in part, an Austrian awareness, but also the difficulties we had in Austria. I still feel fear of the Nazis and of the hard time I spent in prison in Austria. I'm getting back to the head and the heart— the head part is awareness of the misfortune that befell Austria, which turned into a misfortune for the world. But the question is, "How is Austria behaving?" and there, of course, is grave disappointment. The question is, "What lesson has Austria learned from it all?" I have just read some statistics in the Viennese newspaper *Kurier*: According to a survey, the socialists have lost their absolute majority even among the working class. And the truth is that the workers aren't saints either. And I think that even bourgeois democracy has not completely established itself in Austria; Austria has never had a bourgeois revolution. It would be interesting, wouldn't it, to have a bourgeois center party, as they exist in France and in Britain, where the Tories, too, waged war against Hitler with enthusiasm.

Harry Zohn
Boston

Harry Zohn, born November 21, 1923, in Vienna. Attended primary school and Gymnasium (Sperlgasse, 2nd District) until 1938. Escaped to England on February 1, 1938; did not matriculate again until May 1940. Immigrated with his parents to Boston, attended school there until 1941, followed by Suffolk University. Worked as a reporter, 1941–46; undertook doctoral studies at Harvard University, where he received his Ph.D. in 1952. Accepted research post at the German Studies Institute of Brandeis University, 1951. Appointed professor in 1967. Author or translator of 30 books and over 60 articles. Editor or coeditor of numerous scholarly periodicals. Member of Austrian and American PEN, founder of International Arthur Schnitzler Society. Has received numerous orders and distinctions.

I don't believe that any immigrant ever was a burden to his sponsor, or at most was so only in his first week or two. I can say that of our friends who traveled a similar road — all of them have achieved something in America. They became good Americans, and it was only here that they fully developed. Peter Marboe wrote an article in the commemoration year, saying that a man like Harry Zohn was a loss to Vienna University. I retorted that this was nonsense. How could a Jew have got a university post then? In that respect I, or my generation, did all right. This was obvious from the symposium Living with Austrian Literature that was organized in 1988. Those ten invited men and women colleagues all achieved something in America. If there had been no Hitler, if there had been no economic depression, yes, if the little word "if" didn't exist — of course this is all nonsense, but the twenties and thirties were a bad time in Austria.

We arrived in America in June 1940. By the end of the month I was a waiter in a holiday camp, earning tips. I was 16 then. In the autumn I was able to go back to school. I still had my school reports from Vienna, and on the strength of these, even though I hadn't attended any school for two and a half years — from June 1938 to September 1940 — I was immediately put in with my coevals, so that a year later I graduated from high school at age seventeen and a half, moreover with all possible honors. Only then did I realize how good my secondary school in Vienna had been, despite the pressure and despite its authoritarian atmosphere. One really learned something, didn't one? I studied American history, but also typing and shorthand, and I was one of the top students in English. In fact, I was the spelling champion of the whole school. The explanation may not sound plausible, but I had by then mastered the difficult spelling of the English language. I recall the word with which I won — *onerous*. But the teacher mispronounced it and my classmates thought that it had something to do with "honor." But I'd had five years of Latin and knew the word *onus, oneris*, and spelled it correctly. In other words, I very soon proved myself as an American student and graduated from school.

For the rest of the war — from 1941 to 1946 — I was a working student. I worked in an office to pay for my studies in evening classes and summer schools. I had to patch all this together laboriously, at a university that even then was specialized for working students and evening classes. Today I belong to its board of trustees. In 1976 (i.e., 30 years after my studies), it bestowed on me an honorary degree, *Doctor honoris causa*. This is Suffolk University, now a much superior and much bigger institution than during the war. At the time, though, I wanted to be a teacher and attended another university, an hour from here, to get an M.A. in education and teaching.

In 1945, after exactly five years, my parents and I became American citizens in the prescribed minimum period. But over here you enjoy all benefits even without being a citizen. Admittedly, you have to report once a year, at New Year's, and you don't have a vote, but you are free to move around and to earn money.

Did we ever consider, my parents or me, returning to Vienna when the nightmare was over? First of all, it wasn't the same Vienna; our whole circle no longer existed. We had drifted away from Vienna. And, besides, we weren't invited. They didn't do anything to make it easy to go back. If they'd said, "You'll get your apartment back" or "You'll get your business back" — but this didn't happen. You had grown away from it. You knew that the end of the war didn't mean the end of anti–Semitism. Time and again you read that the Austrians weren't going to pay any restitution, that they just hadn't learned anything. We all knew that. My mother was homesick for Vienna, but she wouldn't fly, and by sea it was too complicated. My father had no such wish at all. My mother was sentimental, but my father had become a good American. An American sign-writing entrepreneur. To begin with, he'd worked for some years as a painter-decorator. Then he discovered an advertisement in a paper that there was a sign-writing workshop for sale. He bought it, and subsequently a better and bigger one. He also owned two other firms with a partner and some employees, and he became a well-known Boston sign writer until he retired. After that he became "Grandpa Moses." I have some of his rather primitive flower paintings; he painted picture cards. He was a naive painter and got a lot of pleasure out of it. He lived to the age of 89, my mother to nearly 85.

After the war I wanted to go into teaching. As a *Zohn* (or son) of the German language, I decided I wouldn't be robbed of the language, I wouldn't be robbed of its cultural accomplishments. I have always been interested in literature, which is why I didn't want to be a high school teacher, because that would have meant just language teaching. I wanted to be a scholar. I gave literature courses, I applied for a post at Harvard and immediately got an assistant's post; that was in the autumn of 1947. I was there for four years and completed my doctoral studies more or less in record time. I was teaching all the time, I was myself attending classes, and I found a subject for my thesis that suited me to the ground. I saw myself even then — perhaps still subconsciously — as a mediator between cultures, as a conciliator. Stefan Zweig was an outstanding figure in this respect, and my doctoral thesis, written in English, was on Stefan Zweig as a mediator of European literature.

It has been said of me that I was something of a trailblazer for Austrian literature in this country. I prefer the word mediator. Stefan Zweig was well known for a time, when he had a good publisher and his books appeared in large print-runs. He was certainly better known then than he is today. Now most of his books are out of print and his star has rather faded. I try to work against this trend. Scholarly research really only started to take him seriously since his commemorative year, 1981, when books, dissertations, and such appeared about him.

What does Austria mean to me? Austria is the land of my birth, of my mother tongue. In 1988, quoting Grillparzer, I said in Vienna, "In spite of everything, I am in love with Austria." Not the Austria of Karl Heinrich

Waggerl, of Mirko Jelusich, of Julius Zerzer, or of Gertrud Fussenegger, not a blood-and-soil Austria. I suppose as one gets older, one always looks in literature for oneself. One looks for one's own childhood, for one's own youth. And I am aware of the important role played by the Jews in Austria in the past century, and certainly since the turn of the century.

I have been an American citizen since 1945, but I use every opportunity for going back. The first time was in 1955. I was then a great friend of Hugo Portisch, the head of Austrian radio and television, and he obtained an invitation of the Austrian Press Service as a journalist for me. I wrote a series of seven or eight articles for the *Jewish Advocate* about the Jews in Vienna. And these were a great success. Then I was in Vienna again in 1957 and 1960. And then in 1961, when I became engaged to a young Viennese woman, a Jewish reemigrant from Israel. One reason, I believe, was that I wanted to marry Austria or Vienna again, become part of it. Fortunately for the person concerned this didn't come off. I wanted a European wife at that time; this idée fixe lasted for about a year. Then in 1965 I was there, for the first time, with my Boston wife, through whom I became truly fond of Boston, the best of America. Then in 1971 and 1974 on lecture tours, in 1978 with my wife and both children, who were then quite young. In 1984, my sabbatical semester, I was repeatedly in Vienna, and since then I have been there every year. I was frequently invited, there were symposia — the Karl Kraus symposium, the Beer-Hoffmann symposium — and also lectures. Most recently, in May 1992, I was at the University of Klagenfurt for the symposium on expressionism. I gladly accepted those invitations and enjoyed being there.

Actually, I was never bitter, because I had learned that bitterness is not a very good taste. Bitter, no—but once burnt. I'm not saying this because I am told about a resurgence of anti–Semitism. Well, what did you expect? *The leopard doesn't change his spots.* I knew that the lessons of the Holocaust had not been learned by the world. The Austrians, therefore, are not the only stupid ones. The Austrians are a special case: They are — how shall I put it — like a pampered child. First in November 1943 the Moscow Declaration, then the State Treaty with Austria. The Austrians have more luck than good sense. No wonder, since no one ever pushed their noses into the shit; German noses were pushed in but the Austrian ones were spared. The late Friedrich Torberg, who was a close friend, once wrote that the Austrian form of restitution was "Who cares?" And that's just how it is. And why not? "After all, we were the first to be persecuted, we were the first country Hitler invaded," and so on, and so on. Mind you,

I was an eye witness; I saw what it was like, what labor of love and special efforts the good Austrians made at the time!

When my children were quite small, I spoke only German to them. And they answered me in German, but then there was no support from the social environment; there were no children of their age. None of their young friends knew German, and so it later evaporated. Both children were in Vienna for the first time in 1978. They were a little too young then: My daughter was nine and my son eleven. My daughter takes the Austrian business seriously. My son is going to be a musicologist — he has to read German and of course is concerned with Mozart, the Viennese musicians — but his encounter with Austria is more of an educational experience. In my daughter I observe something more like a primal experience. She went to Vienna in April 1989 on some scheme of the Jewish Welcome Service. That was a marvelous business. Leon Zelman had placed an advertisement that he needed 100 host families for Jewish refugee children, and 1,200 came forward. At that time she also visited Mauthausen, for instance — something I never had the courage to do, although I had ample opportunity. In October 1989, I acted as tour courier for an eleven-day visit by a Jewish women's group. The trip was to Prague, to Budapest, and the third city, of course, was to have been Vienna. There I could have shone as an academic courier, but of course they didn't go to Vienna — because of Waldheim. That's how most Jews are reacting. Many Jewish groups, not only the World Jewish Congress, but much larger groups, stick to this. That is a loss of revenue for Austria, a disaster for the country's tourism — isn't that so?

Lord Weidenfeld
London

Lord Weidenfeld, born as Georg Weidenfeld on September 13, 1919. Attended basic school and Piaristengymnasium in Vienna; graduated in 1937. Attended Konsularakademie (diplomatic academy) beginning in autumn 1937, Kurt Waldheim being a fellow student. Escaped to England on August 8, 1938; together with Nigel Nicolson founded the publishing firm of Weidenfeld and Nicolson. Became a British subject, 1946. In 1949 and 1950, served as chief of staff for Chaim Weizmann, the first president of Israel; continued as his political advisor even after his own return to England. Life peerage 1976 (Lord Weidenfeld of Chelsea); active member of the House of Lords; director of the Weizmann Institute, Israel, and of the Mitchell Foundation, New York. Holder of the Gold Mark of Merit of the Republic of Austria and of the Commander's Cross of the Order of Merit of the Federal Republic of Germany; member of the Légion d'Honneur; Dr.h.c. of the Ben-Gurion University; professor h.c. at St. Peter's College (Oxford); holds numerous other distinctions. Repeatedly married. He has one daughter.

I believe I am something like a result of conciliatoriness, of deliberate compassion. A certain earlier bitterness and a certain hostility have now gone, especially as far as the present nation and ethos of the Austrian Republic is concerned, toward which I have a very positive and admiring attitude. Surely there's no such thing as permanent national characteristics. There's nothing "eternally Austrian"; ultimately there are only atmospheres, attitudes and life philosophies dependent on social, economic, and cultural conditions, and their configuration changes, sometimes very quickly, sometimes subtly. And the Austria I am now talking about, the

Austria of the Second Republic, the Austria of the generation that was born either shortly before or since the Anschluss, this generation, I believe, is a civilized, seriously democratic generation with whom one can live very well and whom one can understand very well.

This attitude developed over the past two decades. Shortly after the war there was, on the part of the exiles, a certain impatience, a skepticism toward Austrian government policy. There was outrage over the lack of restitution and the revival of anti–Semitism, and Austria's distancing itself from Nazism and the Greater Germany idea didn't sound genuine. Over the past 20 years, however, this has become much more convincing and I was able to convince myself, from human relationships and new friendships, that one was really dealing with a new generation and a different mentality.

In my case the issue of returning was never topical. I left because I had to leave. After all, I lived in an atmosphere, as a secondary school pupil and as a student, in which the future was grey; not only was the country grey economically, and with regard to its political future, but I also found myself obstructed as a Jew. There was first the rubber-soled anti–Semitism of the clerical fascists, and then the hobnailed boots of the SS and the SA — that was not a country where you saw a future for yourself. It was an escape for me, and I never for a second considered returning, ever. Added to this was the fact that Britain treated me generously. Austria for me then was something like a museum — festivals, Salzburg, stone and marble, fine museums and churches. At the same time, however, there arose something like pleasure, or even pride, to have grown up in the German linguistic area and with the German mother tongue, and to have always appreciated and cultivated German literature.

Professionally, as a publisher, I have always concerned myself with German and Austrian authors — perhaps more with German. I revisited this cultural landscape time and again, and more and more involved myself in it personally, so that emotionally I reconciled myself with Austria. I never made a secret of this attitude — on the contrary. And because the subject matter is familiar to me, because the history, the culture, the music, and also the politics of Austria have always interested me, I have attempted, out of friendship for Austria — and I hope this doesn't sound condescending — to help the new Austria. Thus, as a member of the British House of Lords, I intervened on the issue of Austria's adherence to the European Economic Community. On the Waldheim affair I have held the view that this was an inflated and tragicomical episode, in which Waldheim was the wrong scapegoat. Certainly the motives of Jewish circles were entirely understandable, but this man simply was the wrong target. This was a case of an accumulated sense of bitterness on the part of many Jews that the Austrians got off so lightly, that, thanks to the Moscow decisions, they suddenly became martyrs and victims, all because of a cynical calculation by the Allies, mainly by the Russians, that this might trigger mass desertions by Austrian members of the Wehrmacht. I said to myself then, yes, they got off very lightly indeed, and it was probably because of this that Austrian governments didn't do much for the Jews. Apparently there were downright anti–Semitic interventions in the Austrian council of ministers on this issue in the forties and fifties. Then suddenly there was the Waldheim affair, which reduced the whole question to one man who, at the age of 22 or 23, was on a sector of the Balkan front — a fact that he had kept silent about or had forgotten to emphasize. The man was 23 years old. Even so, his accusers said, he should have known that four or five miles away some very ugly things were happening; that's possible. I don't wish to acquit him. I only want to say that it was absolutely beyond comparison with other crimes and other persons.

In many aspects of its political culture — assistance with the emigration of Russian Jews via the reception camp of Schönau, its generous asylum policy, the reestablishment of a Jewish community — Austria impressed me favorably. In my life's philosophy, certain harsh, Manichaean contrasts in the assessment and understanding of historical problems have yielded to a rather tolerant, pluralistic assessment of things. Certainly, mistakes were made. I believe that there should have been more emphasis on guilt and on the fact that the little Austria of the twenties and early thirties predominantly regarded itself as part of the German "community of destiny." If, for instance, the Allies had not prevented the customs union with Germany, Austria would probably have become part of the German Reich. There should be no illusions on this point. The Social Democrats were in favor of the Anschluss. And we were, all of us, young Social Democrats. We looked down on the German Party. The middle class, the Agrarian League, the "Greater Germans,"[18] certain groups in the Christian Social movement, and even parts of the Heimwehr, were pro–German; it was really only the Legitimists and some very convinced Christian Social supporters who wanted Austrian independence. [19] They were in the minority. That was one thing. The other was that the Austrian Nazi Party probably included the worst elements of the entire Nazi Party. Surely it was no accident that the SS for Southeast Europe — never mind how —

consisted mainly of Austrians. And in contrast to Prussian anti–Semitism, the one in Austria was a brawling anti–Semitism. All this should have been brought out into the light with much more courage and frankness.

Throughout my life I had a lot to do with politicians and gained much insight into political processes. There is, for instance, the figure of Bruno Kreisky, with whom I didn't get on at all well. He didn't like me and I was very critical of him. Nevertheless I would identify with certain political programs of his. But in many respects, I believe, he went too far. He evidently had to cope with his Jewish origins, and this produced his curious attitude toward the Jews. I'm saying *curious*, though in a sense it was quite traditional because the history of the Jews within the Social Democratic movement has to be seen also as anti–Zionism. And at the same time he was the interesting example of a Jew from Moravia; that is to say, he rather looked *up* to established Viennese Jewry, and looked *down* on the eastern Jews. That was subliminal in him, subconscious. Of course, I didn't share his attitude — I was a Zionist. I was a Zionist from the moment I could no longer legally be a Social Democrat. I was a young lad and a socialist secondary school student of thirteen or fourteen when the Dollfuss revolt took place. And when, like me, you were politically interested at an early age, there wasn't really much choice. You could go underground to the revolutionary socialists or Communists, but I never had a taste for them. There was something distasteful to me about the whole ethos, the ambiance of the Communists — their language, which contained too many foreign words and too many Slavic elements. And the other option was to be Jewish national. The decisive thing was that I happened to encounter a group of young Zionists, who straight away enlisted me for the Jewish student movement, in which I became very active. Perhaps that is why I used to have a great contempt for assimilated Jews. Yes, I really did, but all that has changed a great deal. I continue to be a very active Zionist, but I see the productive features also of other shades of attitudes within the Jewish world, and I regard the whole thing as something like a symphony. One quite simply needs also those who are preserving Jewishness here, and I admit that the new, fresh, virile, and successful Jewish community in Vienna is no thorn in my flesh. One should not regard them as Jews who ought to go to Israel, but one should rejoice in their success and wish them a flourishing prosperity, since everything is *ad majorem gloriam* of the Jewish people. Therefore I am also anxious to see a certain stockade mentality on the part of some Israelis come to an end, for bridges to be built. Especially to Austria, even though it is the land of birth of radical anti–Semitism from Schönerer and Lueger to Hitler. Just as the apostle Peter built a temple in Rome and not in Jerusalem — that is to say in the heart of the enemy country — it would be necessary to apply a lever here, in Austria, by way of conferences, meetings, initiatives, to bring about a new relationship with the Catholic world on the one hand and with the newly opened East on the other. I am still having difficulties about this idea with my Israeli friends, but patience is necessary. And as for Austria, I would wish that it engaged itself intellectually. It could assume a key role in this matter.

Notes

Introduction

1. Their number is approximately 10,000; the percentage of Jews therefore 0.13. Eighty-six percent of those polled put the percentage at two percent or more, up to 10 percent.

2. Stefan Zweig, *Die Welt von Gestern: Erinnerungen eines Europäers* [*The World of Yesterday: Memories of a European*] (Frankfurt: Fischer, 1981), 458. English edition: *The World of Yesterday: An Autobiography*, trans. Cedar and Eden Paul (London, Cassell, 1987).

3. Alfred Polgar, "Der Emigrant und die Heimat," in *Kleine Schriften* [*Minor Writings*], ed. Marcel Reich-Ranicky (Hamburg: Rowohlt, 1982), 238. The reference to "crosses" is to the Catholic underpinnings of Schuschnigg's brand of fascism, whereas "hooked crosses" are swastikas. I am grateful to Klaus Amann for providing this reference.

4. Hilde Spiel, *Rückkehr nach Wien: Ein Tagebuch* [*Return to Vienna: A Diary*] (Munich: Ullstein, 1989), 69. (My translation.)

5. Ed. Alfred Gong, *Interview mit Amerika: 50 deutschsprachige Autoren in der neuen Welt* [*Interview with America: 50 German-Speaking Authors in the New World*] (Munich, 1962).

6. Hermann Broch, *Complete Works,* ed. Paul Michael Lützeler, vol. 13/3 (Frankfurt: Suhrkamp, 1981), 136. (This letter dated March 15, 1947.)

7. Personal communication.

8. Günther Anders, *Die Schrift an der Wand: Tagebücher 1941–1966* [*The Writing on the Wall: Diaries 1941–1966*] (Munich, 1967), October 1950, 163. (My translation.)

9. The British historian Robert Knight was the first person allowed to view the minutes of Austria's postwar cabinet meetings. His special interest was how the federal government treated Jewish claims, how these were deliberately and methodically stymied. In the process, he also documented how anti–Semitic slurs were bandied about by conservatives and Social Democrats alike. For example: Prime Minister Figl (conversation) remarked that "the Jews want to get rich fast … but it is a fact that nowhere does one find so little anti–Semitism as in Austria, and in no other country are the people as tolerant as in ours" (January 14, 1947), while the deputy PM Adolf Schärf opined that "whole regions [of Austria] have been economically devastated by the Jews."

10. Ron Kovic, *Born on the Fourth of July* (New York: Simon & Schuster, 1976), 75.

11. Quoted in Dorit B. Whiteman, *The Uprooted* (New York: Insight Books, 1993), 410.

12. Bertolt Brecht, "Über die Bezeichnung Emigranten," in *Werke*, vol. 12 (Frankfurt: 1988), 81. ("On the Term Emigrants." My translation.)

13. Michael Hubenstorf, "Medizinische Fakultät 1938–1945." *Willfährige Wissenschaft. Die Universität Wien 1938–1945 [Compliant Science: The University of Vienna 1938–1945]*, ed. Gernot Heiss et al. (Vienna: Verlag für Gesellschaftskritik, 1989), 233–282.

14. Lore Segal, *Other People's Houses* (New York: Fawcett Crest, 1964), 25. (First publ. 1958.)

15. Benno Weiser-Varon, *Professions of a Lucky Jew* (New York: Cornwall Books, 1992), 71.

16. Peter Fabrizius, *One and One Make Three: Story of a Friendship* (Berkeley: Ben-mir, 1988), 2.

17. Personal communication, February 1995. The dream, with its elements of sudden disorientation and alienation from fellow citizens, clearly shows the traumatic effect of the Nazi invasion. Edith Arie thought her dream had left her, but it came back during a visit to Austria in the summer of 1994.

18. Cited by Dorit B. Whiteman, *The Uprooted* (New York: Insight Books, 1993), 388.

19. Quoted from a Radio One program on Austrian exiles, March 10, 1998. Later, Feuchtwanger became a successful Hollywood scriptwriter.

20. For this information I am indebted to Edith Mahler-Schachter (cousin to the composer Gustav Mahler), who is now 90 and lives in Bromley, Kent.

21. Vlasta Vizek-Vidovic, "Psychological Aspects of Displacement," in *Psychology and Psychiatry of War,* ed. Eduard Klain (Zagreb Medical Faculty Press, 1992), 165–166.

22. Fritz Beer, in *Die Zeit gibt die Bilder: Schriftsteller, die Österreich zur Heimat hatten[Pictures of Our Time: Authors Whose Homeland Was Austria]*, eds. Alisa Douer and Ursula Seeber, special issue of *Zirkular* (1992), 40.

23. "I encountered among Hiroshima survivors a frequent sense of being 'as-if dead,' or what I called an 'identity of the dead.' ... An expression of this sense of themselves can be found in the lifestyle of many survivors, one of marked constriction and self-abnegation, based on the feeling that any show of vitality is in some way inappropriate for them, not inwardly permissible. They retain a sense of ... guilt and responsibility for the catastrophe itself, despite being victims rather than perpetrators of that catastrophe." Robert J. Lifton, *Boundaries* (New York, Random House, 1969), 13.

24. "I have not yet come across a piece of rape or incest literature that was not published at least ten years after the event." Kali Tal, "A Literature of Trauma," *Fourteen Landing Zones: Approaches to Vietnam War Literature,* ed. Philip K. Jason (Iowa City: University of Iowa Press, 1991), 217–249, fn.6.

25. "Psychoanalysis and the Polis," in *A Kristeva Reader,* ed. Toril Moi (London: Blackwell, 1988), 307.

26. *Scherben sind endlicher Hort. Poems. [Shards Are a Finite Shelter]* (Vienna: Verlag für Gesellschaftskritik, 1991).

Part I: Anti–Semitism Before Hitler

1. Vienna's leading private school, then as today.

2. Weigel (who managed to escape to Switzerland) was one of the few Jewish intellectuals who returned to Vienna after 1945. He was a prominent writer and critic until his death in 1992.

3. Engelbert Dollfuss (b. 1892) was the Austrian prime minister at the time. He overthrew the democratically elected parliament in March 1933 and installed an authoritarian right-wing regime. In July 1934 he was assassinated in a botched Nazi coup.

4. The *Völkischer Beobachter* was the most widely read newspaper during the Nazi era.

5. A province of Upper Austria bordering on Czechoslovakia, 120 miles west of Vienna.

Part II: Anschluss and Escape

1. General Miklós Horthy (1968–1957) was the head of state of Hungary and Hitler's ally. In October 1944 he was deposed by the SS.

2. October 10, 1920, was the date of the post–WWI plebiscite which resulted in a rejection of Serbia's claim to a substantial part of Austria's border region with Slovenia. Prior to the plebiscite, there had been two armed conflicts between local resistance fighters and an invading Serb-Croat-Slovene army.

3. Dachau was the first German concentration camp. It was started in 1933 and at first designated for the detention and torture of political opponents. It lies on the outskirts of Munich. A total of 206,000 inmates passed through it; 32,000 died. Buchenwald was the name for a concentration camp built in 1937, a few miles to the south of Weimar. A total of 239,000 inmates were registered, of whom 56,000 perished. *Buchenwald* simply mean's "beech forest," and that is what the site was, a local forest. The mayor of Weimar had successfully resisted its naming as the "Weimar Concentration Camp," rightly fearing that his city would thus be tainted forever.

4. Then 3,000 schillings was roughly a year's salary for a high school teacher.

5. The 2nd Viennese District was where most working-class and lower-middle-class Jews lived. By 1940, it had been turned into a virtual Jewish ghetto.

6. Bratislava, called *Pressburg* by the Viennese, is located 40 miles down the river Danube. Today it is the capital of Slovakia.

7. Wannsee is a suburb of Berlin. The infamous conference named for it took place on January 20, 1942. It was presided over by Reinhard Heydrich, head of the Gestapo. Hitler had put him in charge to plan the mass extermination of European Jewry with the help of the SS and other organizations. Prior to Wannsee, the Nazi policy had been to force Jews to emigrate.

8. Dr. Kurt Schuschnigg (1897–1972) was the Austrian head of state beginning in 1934, following the assassination of Dollfuss by Austrian Nazis. He handled Hitler's bullying poorly, and as a last-ditch effort to secure Austria's independence, called for a plebiscite scheduled for Sunday, March 13, 1938. Hitler was so enraged by this move that he ordered his troops to invade Austria. Schuschnigg caved and ordered Austrian troops (who were ready to fight) to lay down their arms so as "not to shed any German blood."

9. Often referred to by its German name, *Theresienstadt*, Terezín was a concentration camp in occupied Czechoslovakia. It was started in June 1940 and designed to keep all the Jews of Bohemia and Moravia plus German and Austrian Jews who had distinguished themselves in WWI. Though there were no gas chambers, 35,000 died of malnutrition and diseases. Of a total of 141,000 registered prisoners, 92,000 were deported to Auschwitz and murdered there. Only 14,000 survived.

10. *Rassenschande* (sex between Aryans and Jews) had been declared a criminal offense by the Nuremberg Race Laws in 1935.

11. A Viennese slang term (*a Hetz*) meaning "good fun." It also carries the meaning of "a chase."

12. Hundreds of paintings and other objects were finally auctioned off in October 1996, thanks to an initiative of the Austrian prime minister Vranitzky. The proceeds (155 million schillings) went to Jewish organizations.

13. Oloron is located in southern France. After the defeat of the French army, the southern half of France (Vichy France, named after the city where the treaty was signed) was administered by a puppet regime under General Pétain. Many Jews fled to Vichy France, but many were denounced by collaborators or picked up by German SS.

14. The camp was Drancy, a French transit camp for transports to the Polish death camps. It operated from August 1941 to August 1944. Some 61,000 Jews passed through it; when U.S. troops liberated the camp on August 17, 1944, they found 1,400 survivers.

15. A hill within Vienna's city limits.

Part III: War and Exile

1. Judenburg is a city of about 30,000 inhabitants. Its citizens successfully resisted official attempts to have the name changed. It remained "Judenburg" throughout the Nazi years.

2. A narrow and picturesque section of the valley of the river Enns.

3. The highly toxic cyanide gas used from 1942 in all the death camps.

4. Walter A. Freud has meanwhile returned to Austria three times. He was first invited by a prominent citizen of Zeltweg, where he had attempted to "liberate" the airfield in 1945. He was subsequently also invited to return by the mayor of Vienna.

5. Sir Oswald Mosley (1896–1980), first a Conservative then a Labour MP, founded the British Union of Fascists in 1931. Detained 1940–1943.

6. Bratislava (see fn. 11) had sizable German-speaking and Hungarian minorities before WWII.

7. The minimum age (as of March 1938) for receiving a pension has since been dropped further, to six years.

8. Hitler's mansion near Berchtesgaden. The meeting took place February 12, 1938.

9. The head of the Austrian Nazi Party at the time. In 1940, he was appointed *Gauleiter* (governor) in the occupied Netherlands. Responsible for the deportation of 106,000 Dutch Jews, Seyss-Inquart was tried by the Nuremberg court in 1945 and sentenced to die.

10. The daily newspaper of the Social Democratic Party. Both had been banned by Dollfuss in 1933.

11. Altogether the British government paid out 35,000 pounds in compensation to the victims. A complete account of the matter was provided by Cyril Pearl in his *The Dunera Scandal* (Melbourne: Angus & Robertson, 1983).

12. The death toll was 700.

13. The province was predominantly German-speaking, though a part of Hungary; in 1919 it was given to what was left of Austria (with the exception of its capital, Ödenburg/Sopron).

14. Guido Zernatto was a member of the Schuschnigg Cabinet. He was also a writer and poet.

15. Franz (or Ferenc) Molnar (1878–1952) was a famous journalist, novelist and playwright of Hungarian birth.

16. Ernst Waldinger (1896–1970), Austrian poet.

17. Persecutions against Hungarian Jews were surreptitiously carried out during Horthy's term as regent.

18. *Grossdeutsche Partei.*

19. The Monarchists, called thus because they believed that the exiled Habsburg emperor was the only "legitimate" head of the Austrian state.

Index